# *Your*
# RETIREMENT
# ROADMAP

# Your RETIREMENT ROADMAP

## DON MOORE

*Advantage*®

Published by Advantage, Charleston, South Carolina.
Member of Advantage Media Group.

ADVANTAGE is a registered trademark and the Advantage colophon is a trademark of Advantage Media Group, Inc.

Printed in the United States of America.

ISBN: 978-159932-368-8
LCCN: 2013937116

This publication is designed to provide accurate and authoritative information in regard to the subject matter covered. It is sold with the understanding that the publisher is not engaged in rendering legal, accounting, or other professional services. If legal advice or other expert assistance is required, the services of a competent professional person should be sought.

Advantage Media Group is proud to be a part of the Tree Neutral® program. Tree Neutral offsets the number of trees consumed in the production and printing of this book by taking proactive steps such as planting trees in direct proportion to the number of trees used to print books. To learn more about Tree Neutral, please visit www.treeneutral.com. To learn more about Advantage's commitment to being a responsible steward of the environment, please visit www.advantagefamily.com/green

Advantage Media Group is a publisher of business, self-improvement, and professional development books and online learning. We help entrepreneurs, business leaders, and professionals share their Stories, Passion, and Knowledge to help others Learn & Grow™. Do you have a manuscript or book idea that you would like us to consider for publishing? Please visit advantagefamily.com or call 1.866.775.1696.

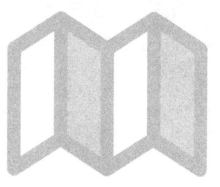

# TABLE OF CONTENTS

# INTRODUCTION

Y ou are on a journey to a place you have never been. That place is retirement. If you were to leave your home today, headed for a physical destination to which you have never been, I am quite confident you would use a roadmap, GPS, trusted directions, or some other material to help you reach that destination in the easiest, shortest, and most comfortable manner. Achieving that manner of journeying toward retirement is what this book is about. If you read and follow the roadmap this book provides, you will find yourself reaching retirement without the worry that the majority of retirees in America have today: Will my money last as long as I do?

If you are reading this book, that means you are at least *thinking* about planning financially for your retirement, which is something woefully few Americans are doing today. More people are already in or approaching retirement than ever before. If that is the case, why are the majority of these folks so poorly prepared for what could and should be the best time of their lives?

There are many answers to that question, and I think I have heard them all. Here are a few sample answers:

- "I do not have time."
- "The government will take care of me."
- "My kids will take care of me."
- "It's too early."
- "It's too late."
- "I have enough money saved in my 401(k)."
- "I am going to keep working as long as I live."
- "I do not know how."
- "Something will happen."

Well, yes, as one answer suggests, something *will* happen, but you probably will not like it—that is, you will not like that something unless you take control of your retirement future. The way things stand now, almost half of America's middle-class workers will be impoverished in retirement, living on a food budget of about $5 a day. That is the sad and shocking reality millions of seniors will face in the not-so-distant future.

You do not have to be one of them.

Through reading this book, you will gain an understanding of why retirement planning is so different today than it was for people in previous generations. You will learn how to invest safely during your retirement years. You will see how all the pieces of your financial picture fit together. You will realize why it is so important to find and work with a trusted retirement income specialist.

There is a sign behind my desk that reads, "Problems seem to bother those the least who plan the most."

Have you been lying awake at night and wondering how you will maintain your lifestyle after you retire? Are you thinking about what might happen if you were to be struck by a debilitating illness? Are you worrying about the next market crash and what it might do to your savings?

If you plan today, I guarantee you will worry less tomorrow.

I am a retirement planner, and I am nearing retirement age myself (that is, I am somewhere between fifty-five and eighty years old, right?). Based on my experience, both as a planner and as a pre-retiree in this country today, we preretirees are in a pickle. The government is in unfathomable debt, the economy is unstable, and the do-it-yourself pension system (e.g., using IRA and 401(k) plans) has clearly failed.

Why? The system has failed because it is based on the expectation that individuals without investment expertise will achieve the same financial results as professional investors and financial advisors would. What results would you expect if a surgeon had to operate on himself? Well, that is where most people are today. The section of the Internal Revenue Code that made 401(k) plans possible was enacted into law in 1978. It was intended to allow taxpayers a break on taxes on deferred income. In 1980, a benefits consultant named Ted Benna took note of the previously obscure provision and figured out that it could be used to create a simple, tax-advantaged way to save for retirement. Over time, companies have moved from pensions that historically provided retirees an income for their life as well as a possible benefit for their spouses to the 401(k) system of retirement. This placed the responsibility on employees to contribute to their own retirement along with a possible percentage match from the employer. The result today is that the average American has a balance of about $60,000 in his or her retirement plan. Little wonder that in a recent survey of retirees the number-one concern is will my money last as long as I do?

The metaphor I use throughout this book is that we preretirees are embarking upon a journey to and through retirement, and we need a reliable roadmap to help us get there safely and securely. We need to know exactly where we are starting, where we are going, and how we can get there while avoiding roadblocks, potholes, hazards, blind spots, and unplanned detours along the way.

This book is an overview, or an introduction, to that journey. Your in-depth map is the direction provided by me, an experienced retirement income expert. I implore you to take action today. Read the book, find a good retirement income planner, and chart your course for retirement. Then, you can start your engine and enjoy the ride!

## Chapter 1:

# YOU ARE HERE

BE PREPARED AND AWARE: YOU ARE FACING A
VERY DIFFERENT LANDSCAPE FROM THAT SEEN
BY PAST GENERATIONS OF RETIREES.

The retirement road today is more complex than ever before. First of all, it is longer and a great deal more crowded. People are living much longer than they did even just a few decades ago. In fact, 50 percent of men who turned sixty-five in 2010 will live to age eighty-one, while 50 percent of women will live to age eighty-four. In addition, roughly 25 percent of men and women are expected to live until ages eighty-seven and ninety, respectively. About a tenth of women today can actually expect to live to age ninety-five.

For the first time in history there are now two living generations of retirees: baby boomers and their parents.

Although longer life expectancy is a wonderful thing, it can present a real issue when people are trying to stretch retirement savings—possibly for thirty years or longer—for income needed to live on and keep up with the constantly rising cost of living. It is not uncommon for retirees today to live as long in retirement as they did in their working years.

When Social Security was established in 1935, the average life expectancy in America was sixty-two. With people scheduled to begin receiving payments at age sixty-five, the program was designed not for the rule, but for the exceptions: the relatively few people at that time who lived to be older than sixty-five.

Over the past several years, estimates of the total size of the public pension problem in the United States have ranged from $730 billion in unfunded liabilities to $4.4 trillion. Many financial economists believe that the true size of the total unfunded liability lies closer to the larger estimates than it does to the smaller.

Now, consider that between now and 2030, it is projected that approximately 10,000 people will turn sixty-five each day. This will increase the number of people eligible for Social Security benefits by 62 percent, while during this time the number of people paying Social Security taxes will increase by only 17 percent. How can the program, which is already operating at a deficit, be expected to serve as a primary source of income for more than 70 million retirees?

It cannot. Here we are in the second decade of the twenty-first century, and Social Security is still playing by a set of rules from the 1940s.

Clearly, Social Security, as we know it, is unsustainable. Meanwhile, pensions, which many people have depended upon for retirement, are fewer and farther between than ever. Only about half of American workers have private pensions, and most of those individuals have seen substantial, defined pension plans replaced by riskier and more limited 401(k) plans. The few traditional pensions remaining are largely underfunded, providing, on average, only 78 percent of the benefits promised.

Reuters' February 8, 2012, coverage of American Airlines' pension default revealed this question and answer:

*"Q. Is the traditional pension as we know it dying?*

*"A. No, but it is hospitalized and on life support. The percentage of Fortune 1000 companies sponsoring an actively accruing pension plan has been dropping sharply for years. The portion in 2011 was 35 percent, down from 59 percent in 2004, according to Towers Watson."*

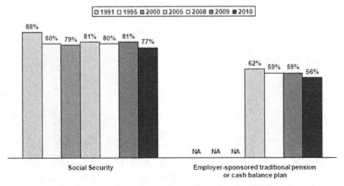

**Workers Expecting Retirement Income From Social Security and Defined Benefit Plans**

Source: Employee Benefit Research Institute and Mathew Greenwald & Associates, Inc., 1991–2010 Retirement Confidence Surveys.

**Source:** Employee Benefit Research Institute

The beginning of the end for pensions began in 1973 with the introduction of 401(k) plans. Since then, more and more employers have shifted the responsibility of pensions from companies to employees. They have said, in essence, to each employee, "Here, you put money in this 401(k) account, and we will match a certain portion of that money."

Money in such accounts, contributed by employees and employers, is invested in a variety of asset categories, such as company stock, money markets, bond funds, index funds, and so on. Yet people holding these accounts have no earthly idea what they are really investing in. They have no guidance. Suppose an employer offers you, as the employee, a 401(k) account. The account comes with a list of choices of where to invest, and you can choose where you want what percentage of your contributions to go. In such a case, you are not sitting down with a financial planner. No one is there to tell you how much risk comes with each investment type. A 401(k) account is a recipe for disaster.

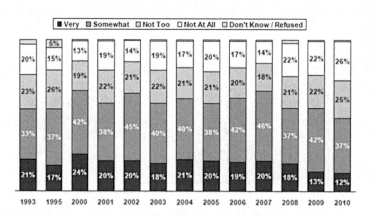

**Worker Confidence in Having Enough Money to Pay for Medical Expenses in Retirement**

Source: Employee Benefit Research Institute and Mathew Greenwald & Associates, Inc., 1993–2010 Retirement Confidence Surveys.

Source: Employee Benefit Research Institute

What if you happen to retire when the market is down? At that point, your retirement savings may be a fraction of what they were when the market was higher. For years, many people were not aware of this potential downfall because their accounts kept going up and up. Then, in 2000, the technology bubble burst; in 2008, the mortgage collapse followed. All too many nest eggs were shattered, forcing many people to delay retirement and many more to re-enter the workforce after retiring.

Even people who followed all the rules—the old rules, that is—have had to set aside their retirement dreams; now they are struggling to make ends meet. The situation is nothing short of tragic. The real tragedy is that many people are still following this same path.

## LONGER LIVES, MORE HEALTH CARE, AND HIGHER COSTS

By living longer, Americans confront potentially crippling health-care costs, and these costs are increasing exponentially as Medicare coverage dwindles. The average retiree will pay $250,000 in out-of-pocket health-care expenses, and this figure does not include long-term care. Unsurprisingly, more than half of workers today doubt they will be able to pay for their health care in retirement.

Even those who retire with employee-sponsored health insurance can accrue substantial health-care bills. To make matters worse, similar to what has happened with lifetime pensions, the number of companies offering retiree health-care benefits is declining. In 1988, 66 percent of companies with two hundred or more employees offered employer-sponsored health insurance to retirees. By 2005, that figure had dropped to 33 percent, according to a Kaiser Family Foundation survey of more than 2,000 employers.

Of course, there is Medicare, which does provide fairly reliable coverage for medically necessary, acute-care issues. However, it is important to know what Medicare does not cover, including hospital stays or doctor visits beyond what the program allows, some prescription medication costs, and a number of other costly services and items, all of which can add up very quickly.

Most importantly, though, you need to understand that Medicare is health insurance, not long-term-care insurance. Let me repeat that:

## MEDICARE IS HEALTH INSURANCE, NOT LONG-TERM-CARE INSURANCE

Medicare may pay for part or all of the medical care provided at a nursing home, such as skilled physical therapy for rehabilitation after surgery or an accident. However, it does not cover custodial care, the type of daily living assistance required by many elderly people.

Before you say, "This will not happen to me," consider this fact: At some point, at least 70 percent of those over sixty-five will need long-term care. The longevity statistics for a healthy couple, both aged sixty-five, indicate that at least one will live to be more than ninety years of age. At least one will most likely spend two to three years in a nursing home, which can easily cost upward of $7,000 a month.

In Chapter 6, you will learn more about long-term care and how to plan for it. For now, though, just be aware that such care is a potentially huge expense that needs to be taken into careful consideration on your retirement roadmap.

## INFLATION, THE INVISIBLE SWINDLER

Health-care costs are rising, and so is the cost of everything else. Assuming an inflation rate of 4 percent, the cost of living will double in nineteen years; this increase in living costs means that an American retiring today will see the purchasing power of his or her retirement savings drop by half during his or her expected lifespan. Today's inflation rate is historically low; a higher rate of inflation will make matters worse.

You might be saying to yourself, "What? Inflation is not at 4 percent right now; it is much lower." Well, yes and no. Anyone who fills up the gas tank or shops at the grocery store on a regular basis knows that prices are climbing faster than 2 percent, which is the annual inflation rate that is currently being reported. What is the reason for this disparity?

Inflation is measured according to the Consumer Price Index (CPI), which takes a number of goods that are representative of the economy and bundles them together in a so-called market basket. The cost of this basket is then compared over time. The problem is that the market basket includes big-ticket items, such as houses, cars, airline fares, college tuition, hospital care, appliances, and computers—things that are not bought very frequently—alongside typical everyday purchases such as food, gasoline, household items, and prescription medication. The price of the large items does not fluctuate nearly as quickly as that of the everyday items, a contrast that flattens out the index results.

In other words, the CPI market basket is rigged to show a lower rate of inflation. The fact that Social Security and many pensions are tied to the CPI means there is a significant lobby out there trying to keep the official rate of inflation as low as possible.

What does all this mean to people on fixed incomes—the people relying on those Social Security and pension checks to get by? This false version of inflation means that these people's loss of purchasing power significantly outpaces the relatively small inflationary adjustments calculated into their monthly Social Security and/or pension income. For some, sadly, this discrepancy can make the difference between going out to dinner once a week and paying the heating bill on time, or between filling the car up with gasoline and buying prescription medication.

Many a retirement plan fails because it does not account for year-over-year inflation; such failing plans trap retirees with drastically reduced purchasing power during a time in their lives when they deserve so much better. Do not put yourself in this unenviable but all too common situation.

## WHERE DOES THIS LEAVE US?

Do not assume for one minute that the government will take care of you after you retire. The U.S. government is up to its eyeballs in debt, reaching $16 trillion at last count, and simply cannot afford to take care of retirees, particularly in light of the senior boom sweeping the country. Retirees are wrestling with a variety of concerns—longevity, unstable markets, health care, and inflation—at the same time that Social Security, Medicare, and economic stability are under siege.

> The bottom line is that you are not going to be provided for unless you take the responsibility of providing for yourself.

How can you be sure that you will not run out of money before you run out of breath? This certainty comes down to three basic elements:

✪ being willing to take action

✪ having personal savings

✪ making top-notch retirement income plans

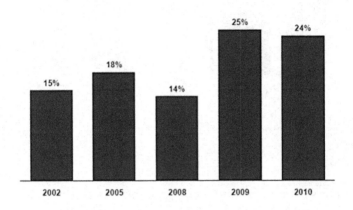

**Workers Reporting They Postponed Their Expected Retirement Age in Past 12 Months**

Source: Employee Benefit Research Institute and Mathew Greenwald & Associates, Inc., 2002–2010 Retirement Confidence Surveys.

Source: Employee Benefit Research Institute

Maybe you have not saved enough for retirement, or maybe you are paralyzed by the potentially overwhelming situation you face. Either way, it is crucial for you to acknowledge your current situation and take immediate action to ensure you will reach your retirement destination of choice.

The other night, I met with a dentist and his wife.[1] At the time of our meeting, Mr. and Mrs. Miller had $1.4 million in savings. They were shocked to learn they were $800,000 short of what they actually needed in order to retire and maintain the lifestyle they desire.

---

1 Throughout the book, I use pseudonyms when referring to clients, people with whom I have worked, or other individuals who appear in examples.

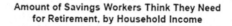

### Amount of Savings Workers Think They Need for Retirement, by Household Income

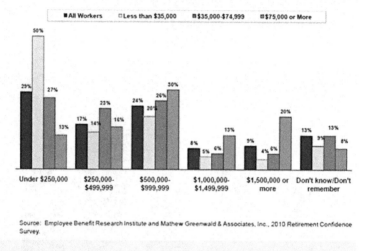

Source: Employee Benefit Research Institute and Mathew Greenwald & Associates, Inc., 2010 Retirement Confidence Survey.

Source: Employee Benefit Research Institute

I am not saying that everyone needs more than $2 million saved for retirement. Instead, I am saying that you have to know how much you will need to maintain the lifestyle you want for the rest of your life. This is not the easiest thing in the world to figure out, but I am here to tell you that it can be done. Figuring this plan out is exactly what we are going to talk about in this book.

The problem is many of us are apathetic. We do not like to think about aging. We do not like to think about our own mortality. Less than 50 percent of people over fifty have actually taken the time to come up with some sort of retirement plan for their future. Even fewer have actually sat down with a professional and put on paper what their retirement years are going to look like.

Why? We do not want to hear bad news. We do not want to talk about things that make us uncomfortable. It is just human nature to put such a discussion off as long as we can.

That kind of procrastination is leading to another sort of delay: Nearly one-quarter of Americans are postponing retirement because they cannot afford it. One-third of Americans age seventy and older are continuing to work because they cannot afford not to do so.

Do not let procrastination steal your tomorrows. Take action now. The reality of where you are today in terms of income and savings might be uncomfortable to face, but trust me, it is a million times better to face that reality than to ignore it.

## HOW MUCH SAVINGS?

How much savings you need for retirement differs greatly by individual or couple. The couple I mentioned before, the Millers, will need about $2.2 million, not just to "get by," obviously, but to maintain the lifestyle they want to have throughout their retirement years.

That situation is at one end of the scale. At the other end are the 43 percent of American workers who have less than $10,000 in retirement savings and the 31 percent who have saved absolutely nothing for retirement. That is right: less than one cent.

Then there is the middle. According to the 401(k) plan records analyzed by the Employee Benefits Research Institute (EBRI), Americans approaching retirement have, on average, three times their annual salaries in their accounts. Without any other form of savings, these retirees will burn through their 401(k) accounts in just seven or eight years; based on life expectancy, they are facing ten or more years with nothing but Social Security income.

Most people do not recognize what a huge problem they may be facing in the not-so-distant future. It is alarming, even heartbreaking, how poorly prepared so many people are in terms of readying their finances to live comfortably throughout their later years.

Now, back to the question at hand. How much money must you save in order to retire? If forced to give you a number out of the blue, I would say you would need a minimum of $500,000. You can also estimate this number based on your annual salary. For example, some financial planners say retirees need anywhere from ten to fifteen times their final annual salaries (the top end of a salary range more amply accommodates the rising costs of health care and the threat of reductions in Medicare and Social Security support).

Suppose you retire at a salary peak of $50,000 per year. Without knowing your particular situation and retirement goals, I would estimate that you would need approximately $500,000 to $750,000 in retirement savings. However, even if you do have that much saved, the amount is not guaranteed to last as long as you do.

Consider this case in point: Recently, Sandra, a seventy-eight-year-old, came in to see me. At the time of our meeting, she had $713,000, all of which was in a brokerage account, and she was spending money according to her wishes. In many cases, people who have that kind of money might not seek any help from a retirement planner. As it turned out, Sandra used to have $1.2 million saved; unfortunately, she took a big hit in 2008 when the market crashed. After going through the experience of losing a sizable chunk of her savings to the whims of the market, she decided to talk to someone with the goal of preventing such a financial loss from happening again. Smart lady.

So, Sandra was seventy-eight years old and had 100 percent of her money at risk in the market. Such a combination is certainly a red flag. A person can put some money at risk like that when he or she is younger, since there is more time for the market to cycle back to a better position if it dips. However, if someone like Sandra has 100 percent of her funds at risk in an unstable market, and has already reached seventy-eight years of age, there is little possibility of recuperating lost funds.

Sandra's other exposure was in long-term care. Even though she already had long-term-care insurance, her plan would only pay up to $100 a day in benefits. That is about half of what long-term care actually costs at present, so she would have to make up the remaining shortfall out of pocket. Paying for the other half of long-term-care costs could eat away at her savings fairly quickly.

At our meeting, I showed Sandra how we could reallocate her assets in safe investments that would guarantee her income for as long as she lives, and we could build in some long-term-care protection to make up for the shortfall in her coverage too.

She liked that plan. Today, she does not have to lie awake at night and worry about the next crash or whether she will be able to afford health care down the road. She can go to sleep knowing that her money is safe and that she will be well cared for if the need arises.

That is what good retirement income planners do. We show people where the potholes are and how to avoid them. We provide options and solutions. We do the math.

Speaking of doing the math, let's turn back to the Millers. At our meeting, after reviewing their assets and expenditures, I showed Mr. and Mrs. Miller that they were $800,000 short of the number they needed to maintain their current lifestyle throughout their retirement years.

Now, I would not tell people they needed that kind of money without showing them some ways to correct the problem. I proposed a variety of solutions to this dilemma.

First, I looked at the Millers' taxes and found they were overpaying by $27,000. They were making the same overpayment every year, which would add up to $270,000 they could have in their pocket over the next ten years and $540,000 over twenty years. (They are in their early sixties and healthy, so planning twenty years ahead is not a stretch.) You might think a taxation mistake like that is rare; believe me, it is not. Almost everyone I see is overpaying his or her taxes; maybe he or she is not overpaying by $27,000 a year, but the number is usually at least $3,000. (We will talk more about taxes in Chapter 4.)

After reviewing the Millers' taxes, I went through their income and expenditures. They had given me a budget that showed they were spending $13,500 a month. However, when I lined their income up against their budget, I noticed $10,000 a month was missing. In other words, the Millers had an extra $10,000 a month coming in compared to what they had going out.

I asked them, "Where's this $10,000 a month going?"

The Millers looked at me like deers in the headlights and said, "Well, we have got no idea."

That might sound crazy to you, but it is not. Here are two smart, successful people who do not have a tight handle on how much money they are actually spending. Again, thinking about how much we spend is something that makes most of us uncomfortable, so we tend to avoid it. Perhaps you would be surprised to learn that when gaps like that are identified and people become more aware of what they spend, it is usually not that hard for them to sharpen their focus and stay within a targeted spending range. Calculating how much you are actually spending is worth doing; by making this calculation, you will give yourself the security of knowing your retirement is safe.

After going through the Millers' taxes, budget, investment statements, insurance policies, and other related materials, I told them they could deal with their retirement savings shortfall in four ways: they could work longer, earn greater investment returns, save more, or spend less.

The Millers did not want to work for a longer period of time. In their case, we were able to change around some investments to get a higher rate of return; plus, the Millers agreed they could spend less and save more. That way, their money would last as long as their life expectancy. Moving forward, they will not have to lower their standard of living; they will just need to be more aware of where their money is going and why.

The Millers have a roadmap, and they are sticking to it. You can too. Just remember this mantra:

> You have to take action to ensure you are heading to your desired retirement destination. I assure you that if you do nothing, you will not like where you end up.

## FACTORS TO CONSIDER

The problem with steady pension benefit checks is that they do not offer the opportunity to increase income sufficiently over the long term. While some pension plans may offer periodic cost-of-living

## LUMP SUMS VERSUS PENSION CHECKS

In recent years, large employers, such as Ford and General Motors, have offered salaried retirees a sizable lump sum in lieu of the steady pension check the retirees had been receiving. In the early summer of 2012, GM offered about 42,000 retirees a lump-sum plan. The retirees had until June 20 to make a decision and up until August 23 to change their minds. By the end of 2013, about 98,000 salaried retirees, former workers, and workers' surviving spouses will have received the same offer from Ford Motors. Recipients of these offers are not required to take the lump-sum option.

This new option could well be the beginning of a trend for many companies that still provide pensions to current employees and retirees. This trend would enable more companies to transition their employ-

increases, an unchanging monthly check loses purchasing power when it is pitted against inflation over time.

Suppose you are trying to choose between a lump sum and a monthly pension. A lump sum could be a good option if you do not expect to live a long time due to the diagnosis of a terminal illness or general poor health combined with a low, familial, life-expectancy rate. Taking a lump sum empowers you with a couple of different options. For one, you can stay on top of medical bills, and perhaps improve your current standard of living, by increasing the amount of money you receive on a regular basis. Second, you can reinvest the lump sum in securities that have a high current level of income. Doing so will still allow you to assign some assets to conservative growth areas and preserve your assets overall.

If you do not need the pension income at present but would like the income to be there for you in the future, taking a lump sum also may be a good decision for you. This choice would allow you to use the money for long-term-growth opportunities that, in turn, would help ensure you have plenty of money in your later years. By taking advantage of such a strategy, you may even be able to leave a larger estate to your loved ones.

In contrast, if you need the income you are receiving from pension payouts, it may be a good idea to maintain the status quo. While retaining your pension means you forfeit the option to reinvest for potentially higher gains, you can appreciate having a reliable source of income and remember that the current

-ees to the more self-directed retirement route. Indeed, figuring out how to position a lump sum to provide income for the rest of one's life is pretty much the ultimate self-directed challenge. If you were ever offered such an option, it would be prudent to consult with an advisor regarding your financial situation before making your decision.

market is not likely to provide you with a guaranteed stream of income that is as high as what you are currently receiving.

When market performance rises again, you may come to question your decision. However, remember that the securities markets flow up and down all the time; generally, in lieu of a salary, having a conservative, guaranteed income is better than having to change standards of living based on the roller-coaster performance of investments. Steady pension paychecks are more likely to provide higher comfort levels and financial confidence.

If you have accumulated an investment-based nest egg, continuing your pension may enable you to be significantly more aggressive with your portfolio than you could be if you had to rely on it for retirement income. The security of pension paychecks frees you to invest in stocks, bonds, and other assets, thereby mitigating the impact of long-term inflation. You can then use this nest egg to supplement your pension and Social Security income, and you can also use it to pay for unexpected or expensive items you need or desire throughout retirement.

Joshua Gotbaum, the director of the Pension Benefit Guaranty Corporation, has recommended that current retirees should not swap a pension for a lump sum. In his words, doing so is like asking yourself, "Why don't you stop being a retiree and start becoming a professional investor?"

........................................................................................

[END OF CHAPTER WRAP-UP]

# YOU ARE HERE

- ✪ The retirement landscape is much more daunting than it once was, due to a variety of reasons:

    - People are living longer, which greatly extends retirement needs.

    - A huge national debt means the government will provide decreasing support to a rapidly growing, aging population.

    - Increasingly fewer employers provide pensions to employees (and some are failing to honor them).

    - The cost of health care, a significant need among retirees, is skyrocketing.

    - The rising prices of other essentials, such as food and fuel, coupled with inflation, are steadily eroding purchasing power.

    - Global economic uncertainty makes for investment uncertainty and confusion.

- ✪ You are not going to be provided for unless you take the responsibility of providing for yourself. Doing so includes finding a knowledgeable guide to help you get where you want to be in retirement.

✪ Maybe you have not saved enough for retirement, or maybe you are paralyzed by the potentially overwhelming situation you face. Either way, it is crucial for you to acknowledge your current situation and take immediate action to ensure you will reach your chosen retirement destination.

*Chapter 2:*

# DEFINE YOUR DESTINATION

YOU HAVE TO KNOW WHERE YOU ARE
GOING TO TAKE THE RIGHT ROUTE.

Entering retirement does not correspond to entering some nebulous dreamland. As a retiree, you face day-to-day life with day-to-day needs, just as you did before. The main difference is that you will not have a regular paycheck coming in. You will have Social Security benefits and, perhaps, a pension. However, typically, these funds represent only one-third to two-thirds of what you were bringing in while you were working. That leaves a significant income gap. A retirement income planner's job is to show you how to leverage your savings most effectively and close that gap with guaranteed lifetime income.

Yes, that goal really is attainable; in fact, helping people achieve it is what I do every day. When I first sit down with people, I find

Half of the U.S. workers who are at least forty-five years old have never tried to calculate how much money they will need to live comfortably in retirement.

there is usually one overarching objective they have in common: "I want to live well in retirement and have my money last as long as I do."

Okay, that desire is fair enough. However, to chart out a path for getting to that broad destination, we first have to find out a person's *specific* goals and priorities along the way. For example, here are some of the retirement wishes people have:

- ✪ "I want to stay in my home for the foreseeable future."

- ✪ "I want to move to a smaller home in a retirement community."

- ✪ "Retiring at age sixty-two is a priority for me."

- ✪ "I want to keep working as long as I can."

- ✪ "I'd like to start a part-time consulting business after I retire."

- ✪ "I plan to do volunteer work in the community."

- ✪ "I have several rental properties. I either need to sell them in the most profitable and tax-efficient way or pass them along to my children before I get too old to manage them."

- ✪ "We'd like to help pay for our grandchildren's education."

- ✪ "We have always dreamed of having a houseboat. Would that be feasible?"

✪ "I want to make sure my spouse has plenty of money if I die first."

✪ "When we die, we want our estate to pass on to our children without probate or excessive taxes."

✪ "If I become disabled, I want to make sure I can afford the care I need so I am not a burden to my family."

✪ "I need flexibility in my retirement plan in case something unexpected comes along."

The list can—and should—go on and on. My point is this: To chart out a successful retirement roadmap, you first need to tackle the following:

✪ Define your specific goals and priorities.

✪ Estimate as closely as possible the costs and/or income associated with each goal.

✪ Identify a time frame for each goal.

In turn, a good retirement income planner can translate your retirement dreams into a tangible strategy for making those dreams come true. Bear in mind that unless you have unlimited—or at least rather extensive—resources, coming up with a realistic strategy will probably require some give-and-take.

Let's return to the example from Chapter 1. After running their numbers, I told the Millers they would need to make some changes to achieve their goal of maintaining their current lifestyle in retirement. As is typical in these cases, the Millers' solution involved a combination of actions, including reallocating some assets to achieve higher rates of return, saving a specified amount of money each month, and holding expenditures to a specified amount each month. For the Millers, these actions were realistic and doable.

Of course, that same strategy is not going to work for everyone. Let's look at another example. The Russells are in their midfifties. They are both still working and have a combined income of $102,000 a year. When I crunched their numbers, I found they had four possible single options:

**Option 1:** Their investments would have to yield a totally unrealistic 12 percent a year to make up their retirement income shortfall. This is not possible.

**Option 2:** They would need to save an additional $44,000 a year until retirement in order to maintain their current standard of living in retirement and have it last as long as their life expectancy. That is a completely impractical scenario. Nobody could manage to save 44 percent of his or her income.

**Option 3:** They could cut their spending to $54,000 a year in retirement, but that would mean downgrading their standard of living to half of their accustomed standard, which is a very drastic change.

**Option 4:** They could continue saving and spending as they had been, but work until they turned seventy-five.

As you can see, none of these options seemed very feasible on its own. However, we were able to come up with a combination of the four that worked for the Russells. For instance, they will be able to maintain their standard of living and have their money last through their life expectancy of age eighty-five by combining these three tactics: realigning their investment portfolio to increase the rate of return to 7.75 percent; saving an additional $1,000 a month (and investing it at that 7.75 percent); and working until age sixty-seven, rather than their original retirement target age of sixty-six.

As is often the case, the Russells had to rebalance some of their expectations against their pocketbook. However, is it not better for them to be aware of this dynamic now, while they are still in their midfifties, than waiting until their options run out? You bet it is.

## THE NITTY-GRITTY

A guaranteed-for-life income strategy is only as reliable as the information that goes into formulating that strategy. That is why I work with clients to gain as much insight as possible into each person's specific situation. As described above, understanding each person's retirement goals and priorities is fundamental to crafting a sound retirement plan. So too is collecting comprehensive data about all financial aspects of each client's life.

To show you the level of detail required, on the next few pages I have included the data intake form I use to gather clients' information. Keep in mind that I am not showing you this form to scare you off. On the contrary, I am including the form to help get you thinking about the level of detail and work that you need to put into a comprehensive retirement plan.

Name _____

Date _____

# PERSONAL FINANCIAL DATA FORM

**Your Personal Analysis will help determine:**

- Whether or not your assets are properly positioned.
- If your present method of savings and investment makes maximum use of your pre-tax and after-tax income.
- How much capital you will need to produce a comfortable retirement income.
- The kinds of savings and investments you will need to reach your goals.
- How much you should set aside each month for savings and investments.
- The potential effects of inflation on your savings and investments.
- The kind of tax-advantaged investments best suited to your needs.
- The monthly income your family will need in the event of your premature death.
- The amount and type of life and disability insurance you need.

# Personal Financial Data Form Introduction

Congratulations on taking the first step toward reaching your goals! It has been said, "a journey of a thousand miles begins with a single step." Completing this data form is your first step toward achieving your goals.

Before you begin you need to have a clear idea of where you are. This data form is designed to simplify, as much as possible, the gathering of your financial information. The analysis that comes from this data may provide the basis for making recommendations for specific investments and other financial tools that you may consider to help meet your family's needs and achieve your goals. This analysis can only be as accurate as the information you provide.

When entering amounts, use only whole dollar numbers. If you want additional information about a particular section please call the office, or write "Please Call" in the margin or "Notes" section and you will be contacted prior to your appointment. If you prefer, you may supply copies of statements in lieu of completing the corresponding sections. If there is not enough space in a section, please make a copy of the page and clearly indicate the attachment.

**Information considered critical for completing the analysis is highlighted in gray.**

## FAMILY DATA

| | First Name | M.I. | Last Name | Birth Date | Sex | Social Security No. | Smoker |
|---|---|---|---|---|---|---|---|
| Client A | | | | __/__/__ | __ | | ☐ Y ☐ N |
| Client B | | | | __/__/__ | __ | | ☐ Y ☐ N |

Home Address: Street _____

City _____ State _____ Zip _____

Home Phone: ( _____ ) _____  Home Fax: ( _____ ) _____

Business Phone:
Client A ( _____ ) _____  Client B ( _____ ) _____

Business Fax:
Client A ( _____ ) _____  Client B ( _____ ) _____

E-Mail Address:
Client A _____  Client B _____

## DEPENDENTS

Please list all children and indicate if they are dependent.

| | Name | Birth Date | Sex | Dependent of | College Choice* | Start Age | Years in School | % Cost You Must Pay |
|---|---|---|---|---|---|---|---|---|
| Children: | | __/__/__ | | ☐ A ☐ B | | | | |
| | | __/__/__ | | ☐ A ☐ B | | | | |
| | | __/__/__ | | ☐ A ☐ B | | | | |
| | | __/__/__ | | ☐ A ☐ B | | | | |
| | | __/__/__ | | ☐ A ☐ B | | | | |
| Others: | | __/__/__ | | ☐ A ☐ B | | | | |
| | | __/__/__ | | ☐ A ☐ B | | | | |

* **College Choice:** If a choice has not been made, simply enter the type of education planned (public or private) and the approximate cost for the dependent. If you do not want to fund college or education needs enter *"None."*

Notes: _____

## OCCUPATION

| | Occupation | Employer | Date Started | |
|---|---|---|---|---|
| Client A | | | __/__/__ | ☐ Retired ☐ Self-Employed |
| Client B | | | __/__/__ | ☐ Retired ☐ Self-Employed |
| Notes: | | | | |

## INCOME

List annual income or attach W2's and paycheck stubs.

If joint, use "Client A" column.

| Source | Client A | Client B | Source | Client A | Client B |
|---|---|---|---|---|---|
| Salary & Wages | | | Social Security Benefits | | |
| Net Self-Employment | | | IRA/Keogh Withdrawals | | |
| Taxable Interest | | | Taxable Pension Income | | |
| Tax Exempt Interest | | | Taxable Annuity Income | | |
| Dividends | | | Non-taxable Income | | |
| Alimony Received | | | Tax-free Income | | |
| Capital Gains | | | Other | | |
| Rental Property Income | | | Other | | |
| Royalty Income | | | Other | | |
| Partnership Income | | | Other (non cash flow) | | |
| Income from Trusts | | | Expected Salary Increase | % | % |

Notes:

## TAXES

List last year's annual tax information or attach Income Tax Return(s).

| Information | Client A | Client B |
|---|---|---|
| IRA Deduction | | |
| Keogh/SEP Deduction | | |
| Qualified Plan Contributions (401k, Profit Sharing, etc.) | | |
| (Section 457) | | |
| Alimony Paid | | |
| Other Adjustments | | |
| Standard Deductions | ☐ | ☐ |
| Itemized Deductions | | |
| Tax Credits | | |

**Filing Status**

Client A .............. ☐ Married/Joint   ☐ Single
                      ☐ Married/Separate   ☐ Head of Household

Client B .............. ☐ Married/Joint   ☐ Single
                      ☐ Married/Separate   ☐ Head of Household

**Prior Year Taxes:**

| | |
|---|---|
| Federal Income | |
| State Income | |
| Local income | |
| FICA | |
| Property | |
| Other | |

Notes:

## BUDGET

| | Monthly Amount | | Monthly Amount |
|---|---|---|---|
| Food | | Automobile Expenses & Leases | |
| Medical/Dental | | Rent | |
| Entertainment | | Education Expenses | |
| Charity/Gift Giving | | Other | |
| Clothing | | Other | |
| Home Maintenance | | Other | |
| Utilities | | Total | |
| Business Expenses | | Additional Amount You Could Save | |

Notes:

## DEBTS/LIABILITIES

List debts/
liabilities
other than
real estate.

| Description | Owner* | Original Amount | Original Date | Term | Current Balance | Payment Amount | Payments Remaining | Int. Rate | Insur-ance** |
|---|---|---|---|---|---|---|---|---|---|
| | | | _/_/_ | | | | | | |
| | | | _/_/_ | | | | | | |
| | | | _/_/_ | | | | | | |
| | | | _/_/_ | | | | | | |
| | | | _/_/_ | | | | | | |
| | | | _/_/_ | | | | | | |
| | | | _/_/_ | | | | | | |

* **Owner:** Enter the abbreviation that applies to the **liability**: A-Client A, B-Client B, or C-Joint.

** **Insurance:** Enter **L** for Life Insurance, or **D** for Disability Insurance on this liability. If both, enter **LD**.

Notes: _____

## MONEY OWED YOU

| Description | Owner* | Original Amount | Original Date | First Payment | Current Balance | Int. Rate | Payment Amount | Term |
|---|---|---|---|---|---|---|---|---|
| | | | _/_/_ | _/_/_ | | | | |
| | | | _/_/_ | _/_/_ | | | | |
| | | | _/_/_ | _/_/_ | | | | |
| | | | _/_/_ | _/_/_ | | | | |
| | | | _/_/_ | _/_/_ | | | | |

* **Owner:** Enter the abbreviation that applies to the **money owed you**: A-Client A, B-Client B, J-Joint Tenants, C-Tenants-in-Common, **CP**-Community Property, **U**-UTMA Uniform Transfer to Minors Act, **T**-Trust.

Notes: _____

## ANTICIPATED FUTURE INCOME

Include
future
income from
trusts and
inheritances.

| Description | Amount | Rate of Increase | Taxable | Tax Basis | Lump or Annual | Start Year | End Year | Owner* | Spend % | Invest % |
|---|---|---|---|---|---|---|---|---|---|---|
| | | | □Y □N | | | | | | | |
| | | | □Y □N | | | | | | | |
| | | | □Y □N | | | | | | | |
| | | | □Y □N | | | | | | | |
| | | | □Y □N | | | | | | | |

* **Owner:** Enter the abbreviation that applies to the **anticipated future income**: A-Client A, B-Client B, or J-Joint Tenants.

Notes: _____

## RETIREMENT ASSUMPTIONS

Desired **Monthly, After-Tax Retirement Income** (in today's dollars) ........................................

Average Annual Inflation Rate ...................................................................................... _____ %

| Retirement Considerations | Client A | Client B | | Client A | Client B |
|---|---|---|---|---|---|
| Planned Retirement Age ........ | | | Are you eligible to participate in an employer-sponsored retirement plan? | □Y □N | □Y □N |
| Do you want Social Security included as a retirement income source? .................. | □Y □N □ Not Eligible □ Reduced____% | □Y □N □ Not Eligible □ Reduced____% | Are you a participant in the Federal Employees Retirement System or Railroad Retirement Plan? | □Y □N | □Y □N |

Notes: _____

## RETIREMENT PLANS

Account information and holdings.

**Plan A** Description: _____ Plan:* _____ Owner:** _____ Beneficiary:** _____

| Plan A Investments | Type *** | Value | Total Return | Cash Yield | Annual Additions (indicate $ or %) | |
|---|---|---|---|---|---|---|
| | | | | | Client | Employer |
| | | | | | | |
| | | | | | | |
| | | | | | | |
| | | | | | | |

**Plan B** Description: _____ Plan:* _____ Owner:** _____ Beneficiary:** _____

| Plan B Investments | Type *** | Value | Total Return | Cash Yield | Annual Additions (indicate $ or %) | |
|---|---|---|---|---|---|---|
| | | | | | Client | Employer |
| | | | | | | |
| | | | | | | |
| | | | | | | |
| | | | | | | |

**Plan C** Description: _____ Plan:* _____ Owner:** _____ Beneficiary:** _____

| Plan C Investments | Type *** | Value | Total Return | Cash Yield | Annual Additions (indicate $ or %) | |
|---|---|---|---|---|---|---|
| | | | | | Client | Employer |
| | | | | | | |
| | | | | | | |
| | | | | | | |
| | | | | | | |

**Plan D** Description: _____ Plan:* _____ Owner:** _____ Beneficiary:** _____

| Plan D Investments | Type *** | Value | Total Return | Cash Yield | Annual Additions (indicate $ or %) | |
|---|---|---|---|---|---|---|
| | | | | | Client | Employer |
| | | | | | | |
| | | | | | | |
| | | | | | | |
| | | | | | | |

**Plan E** Description: _____ Plan:* _____ Owner:** _____ Beneficiary:** _____

| Plan E Investments | Type *** | Value | Total Return | Cash Yield | Annual Additions (indicate $ or %) | |
|---|---|---|---|---|---|---|
| | | | | | Client | Employer |
| | | | | | | |
| | | | | | | |
| | | | | | | |
| | | | | | | |

\* **Plan:** Enter the abbreviation that applies to **qualified plan type**: I-IRA, K-Keogh, P-Profit Sharing/401k, S-SEP-IRA/Simple, T-TSA/403b, D-Deferred Comp/457, O-Other, R-Roth IRA.

\*\* **Owner** and **Beneficiary:** Enter the abbreviation that applies to the **owner or beneficiary of this qualified plan**: A-Client A, B-Client B, CHI-Child, CHA-Charity, O-Other .

\*\*\* **Type:** Enter the abbreviation for **each holding in this retirement account**: C-Cash Holding, B-Bond, S-Stock, M-Mutual Fund, U-Unit Investment Trust, LP-Limited Partnership, T-Tangible Asset.

**Notes:** _____
_____
_____

## PENSIONS

↻ Defined benefit plans.

| Description | Partici-pant* | Monthly Benefit | Increase % | Benefits Start at Age | Death Benefit** | | |
|---|---|---|---|---|---|---|---|
| _____ | ___ | ___ | ___ | ___ | ___ | / ☐ Lump Sum | ☐ Monthly |
| _____ | ___ | ___ | ___ | ___ | ___ | / ☐ Lump Sum | ☐ Monthly |
| _____ | ___ | ___ | ___ | ___ | ___ | / ☐ Lump Sum | ☐ Monthly |

\* **Participant:** Enter the **client the pension applies to**: **A**-Client A, **B**-Client B.

\*\* Indicate after amount if death benefit is a **L**-lump sum or **M**-monthly payment.

**Notes:** _____

_____

## INVESTMENT ASSETS

↻ List all investment assets or attach statements.

| Name/Description | Type * | Owner ** | Value | Total Return | Cash Yield | Annual Additions |
|---|---|---|---|---|---|---|
| Checking Account | C | ___ | ___ | ___ | ___ | ___ |
| Money Market | C | ___ | ___ | ___ | ___ | ___ |
| Savings | C | ___ | ___ | ___ | ___ | ___ |
| Certificate of Deposit | C | ___ | ___ | ___ | ___ | ___ |
| | | ___ | ___ | ___ | ___ | ___ |
| | | ___ | ___ | ___ | ___ | ___ |
| | | ___ | ___ | ___ | ___ | ___ |
| | | ___ | ___ | ___ | ___ | ___ |
| | | ___ | ___ | ___ | ___ | ___ |
| | | ___ | ___ | ___ | ___ | ___ |
| | | ___ | ___ | ___ | ___ | ___ |
| | | ___ | ___ | ___ | ___ | ___ |

\* **Type:** Enter the abbreviation for each **investment asset**: **C**-Cash Holding, **B**-Bond, **S**-Stock, **M**-Mutual Fund, **U**-Unit Investment Trust, **LP**-Limited Partnership, **T**-Tangible Asset.

\*\* **Owner:** Enter the abbreviation that applies to the owner of these investment assets: **A**-Client A, **B**-Client B, **J**-Joint Tenants, **C**-Tenants-in-Common, **CP**-Community Property, **U**-UTMA Uniform Transfer to Minors Act, **T**-Trust.

**Notes:** _____

_____

## INVESTMENT ATTITUDES

**Circle your opinion:** ❶ Strongly Disagree ❷ Disagree ❸ Neutral ❹ Agree ❺ Strongly Agree

| Statement | Opinion |
|---|---|
| I am willing to hold my investments in my portfolio for at least five years. | 1 2 3 4 5 |
| It is important that I am able to convert my investments into cash on short notice. | 1 2 3 4 5 |
| I am concerned that inflation may erode the value of my investments. | 1 2 3 4 5 |
| I am comfortable holding onto an investment during market fluctuations in order to achieve long-term objectives. | 1 2 3 4 5 |
| I am uncomfortable with the possibility that my portfolio may lose value. | 1 2 3 4 5 |
| It is important that my portfolio earns the highest overall rate of return possible. | 1 2 3 4 5 |
| I do not need current income from my investments. | 1 2 3 4 5 |
| It is important that my portfolio generates the maximum amount of income possible. | 1 2 3 4 5 |
| I am most comfortable when my portfolio contains many different investments. | 1 2 3 4 5 |
| Tax-advantaged investments are very important to me. | 1 2 3 4 5 |

## ANNUITIES

List annuities or attach statements.

| Company Name | Annui- tant* | Type ** | Owner * | Payout Amount | Cash Value | Total Return | Payout Type*** | Benefi- ciary **** | Annual Additions |
|---|---|---|---|---|---|---|---|---|---|
| | | | | | | | | | |
| | | | | | | | | | |
| | | | | | | | | | |
| | | | | | | | | | |

* **Owner** and **Annuitant:** Enter the abbreviation that applies to the **annuity**: **A**-Client A, **B**-Client B, **O**-Other, **J**-Joint Tenants, **C**-Tenants-in-Common, **CP**-Community Property, **U**-UTMA Uniform Transfer to Minors Act, **T**-Trust.

** **Type:** Enter the abbreviation that applies to the **type of annuity**: **F**-Fixed, **V**-Variable.

*** **Payout Type:** Enter the abbreviation for the **type of annuity payouts**: **I**-Immediate, **D**-Deferred.

**** **Beneficiary:** Enter the abbreviation that applies to the **beneficiary**: **A**-Client A, **B**-Client B, **CHI**-Child, **CHA**-Charity, **O**-Other.

Notes: _____

## BUSINESS ASSETS

| Description | Owner* | Value | Cost Basis | Cash Yield | Growth Rate |
|---|---|---|---|---|---|
| | | | | | |
| | | | | | |

* **Owner:** Enter the abbreviation that applies to the **business asset**: **A**-Client A, **B**-Client B, **J**-Joint Tenants, **C**-Tenants-in-Common, **CP**-Community Property, **U**-UTMA Uniform Transfer to Minors Act, **T**-Trust.

Notes: _____
_____

## REAL ESTATE  Section One: Property information

| Description | Type * | Owner ** | Purchase Price | Market Value | Improve- ments | Property Tax | Growth Rate | Cash Yield | Insur- ance *** |
|---|---|---|---|---|---|---|---|---|---|
| A. | | | | | | | | | |
| B. | | | | | | | | | |
| C. | | | | | | | | | |

* **Type:** Enter an abbreviation for the **property type**: **P**-Primary, **S**-Secondary, **R**-Recreational, **I**-Investment, **RNT**-Rental, **O**-Other.

** **Owner:** Enter the abbreviation that applies to the real estate: **A**-Client A, **B**-Client B, **J**-Joint Tenants, **C**-Tenants-in-Common, **CP**-Community Property, **U**-UTMA Uniform Transfer to Minors Act, **T**-Trust.

*** **Insurance:** Enter **L** for Life Insurance, or **D** for Disability Insurance on this property. If both enter **LD**.

Notes: _____
_____

## REAL ESTATE  Section Two: Mortgage information for properties listed above

| | Original Amount | Payment Amount | Current Balance | Original Date | Monthly Payment | Term Years | Interest Rate | Type * |
|---|---|---|---|---|---|---|---|---|
| A. | | | | _/_/_ | | | | |
| B. | | | | _/_/_ | | | | |
| C. | | | | _/_/_ | | | | |

* **Type:** Enter **A** for Adjustable, or **F** for fixed.

Notes: _____
_____

## LIFE INSURANCE

➲ List policies or attach statements.

| Company Name | Insured * | Type ** | Owner * | Death Benefit | Cash Value | Rate of Return | Premium | Mode *** | Loan Amount | Loan Rate | Benefi-ciary* |
|---|---|---|---|---|---|---|---|---|---|---|---|
| | | | | | | | | | | | |
| | | | | | | | | | | | |
| | | | | | | | | | | | |
| | | | | | | | | | | | |
| | | | | | | | | | | | |

\* **Insured**, **Owner**, and **Beneficiary:** Enter the abbreviation that applies to the **life insurance policy**: **A**-Client A, **B**-Client B, **CHI**-Child, **CHA**-Charity, **O**-Other, **J**-Joint Tenants, **C**-Tenants-in-Common, **CP**-Community Property, **U**-UTMA Uniform Transfer to Minors Act, **T**-Trust.

\*\* **Type:** Enter the abbreviation that applies to the **type of insurance**: **GT**-Group Term, **T**-Term, **W**-Whole Life, **U**-Universal, **V**-Variable, **VU**-Variable Universal.

\*\*\* Enter an abbreviation for the **premium payment mode**: **A**-Annual, **S**-Semi-annual, **Q**-Quarterly, or **M**-Monthly.

**Notes:** _____
_____

## OTHER INSURANCE

| Type | Owner* | Premium | Mode ** | Benefit | Annual Increase | Waiting Period | Max. Benefit Period |
|---|---|---|---|---|---|---|---|
| Disability | | | | | | | |
| Disability | | | | | | | |
| Long-Term Care | | | | | | | |
| Long-Term Care | | | | | | | |
| Other | | | | | | | |
| Other | | | | | | | |
| Auto Insurance | | | | | | | |
| Auto Insurance | | | | | | | |
| Home Owners | | | | | | | |
| Medical Insurance | | | | | | | |

\* **Owner:** Enter the abbreviation that applies to the **insurance policy**: **A**-Client A, **B**-Client B

\*\* Enter an abbreviation for the **premium payment mode**: **A**-Annual, **S**-Semi-annual, **Q**-Quarterly, or **M**-Monthly.

**Notes:** _____
_____

## GOALS

| Name/Description | Amount Needed | Frequency* | First Payment | Number of Payments | Amount Saved |
|---|---|---|---|---|---|
| | | | __/__/__ | | |
| | | | __/__/__ | | |
| | | | __/__/__ | | |
| | | | __/__/__ | | |
| | | | __/__/__ | | |

\* Enter an abbreviation for the **payment frequency**: **L**-Lump sum, **A**-Annual.

**Notes:** _____
_____
_____

## ESTATE PLANNING

**Estate Planning Information**

|  | Client A | Client B | Joint |
|---|---|---|---|
| Simple Will | _/_/_ | _/_/_ | |
| Durable Power of Attorney | _/_/_ | _/_/_ | |
| Lifetime Gifts | $ _____ | $ _____ | $ _____ |
| Value of Personal Property | $ _____ | $ _____ | $ _____ |
| Estimated Final Expenses | $ _____ | $ _____ | |

Provide any information which will help in determining your estate taxes and life insurance needs

**Desired Monthly, After-Tax Survivor Income** $ _____ .  To use current budget information, check here. ☐

If you have varying survivor income objectives based upon family circumstances, enter details here:

| Beginning Year | How Long | Explanation* | Amount |
|---|---|---|---|
| _____ | _____ | _____ | _____ |
| _____ | _____ | _____ | _____ |
| _____ | _____ | _____ | _____ |
| _____ | _____ | _____ | _____ |

\* Enter any additional information which may help in determining appropriate survivor income needs including person's name, specific ages, or events (include year).

**Notes:** _____

_____

## ESTATE DISTRIBUTION

**Desired Estate Distribution**

What provisions have you made for distributing your estate?

|  | Client A | Client B |
|---|---|---|
| *Enter Values in the following fields as either Dollar Amounts or Percentages* | | |
| Spouse | _____ | _____ |
| Qualified Terminable Interest Property (QTIP or QDOT) | _____ | _____ |
| Credit Shelter or Bypass Trust | _____ | _____ |
| Generation Skipping Trust | _____ | _____ |

Does your will make any direct bequests?

|  | Client A | Client B |
|---|---|---|
| To Family Members | _____ | _____ |
| To Other (non-family) | _____ | _____ |
| To Charity | _____ | _____ |

Does your will make any additional bequests at the last death?

|  | Last Death |
|---|---|
| *Enter Values in the following fields as Dollar Amounts* | |
| To Non-family (other) | _____ |
| To Charity | _____ |

**Notes:** _____

_____

Use this space to provide us with additional information or comments.

_____
_____
_____
_____
_____
_____
_____
_____

## ASK YOURSELF ...

Are you overwhelmed? Don't be. Yes, the previous pages may seem intimidating, both in the depth of detail requested and in the breadth of areas covered. Rest assured, though, that a top-notch retirement-income planner can analyze this information and determine the following:

- whether or not your assets are properly positioned
- if your present method of saving and investing makes maximum use of your pretax and post-tax income
- how much capital you will need to produce a comfortable retirement income
- the kinds of savings and investments you will need to achieve your goals
- how much you should set aside each month for savings and investments
- the kind(s) of tax-advantaged investments best suited to your needs
- the monthly income your family will need in the event of your death
- the amount and type of life and disability insurance you need

Can you imagine the peace of mind that comes with having the answers to these questions? There will be no more uncertainty and no more waking up in the middle of the night wondering, "What if?" You will have no more questions about where your retirement journey will lead you because you will know exactly where you are going and how you will get there.

# DEFINE YOUR DESTINATION

✪ The first part of retirement planning is defining your goals and projecting the costs associated with those goals. Make sure to factor inflation estimates and healthcare expenses not covered by Medicare into the projected costs.

✪ Next, look at income. Are your Social Security and pension benefits enough to cover the expenses you have identified? If not, you have an *income shortfall.* That is a situation in which your savings and investments must come in to bridge the gap between your *income number* (the amount of money you need to support your lifestyle) and your *income reality* (incoming money from Social Security, pension, part-time work, rentals, and so on).

✪ After running the numbers, you might have to rebalance your expectations against your pocketbook. Early retirement might not be financially feasible, for example, or extensive travel every year might be too extravagant. You are better off identifying such issues now, however, than after retirement, when it is too late.

# *Chapter 3:*

## AGE MATTERS

There is a cavernous difference between preretirement financial planning and postretirement financial planning. In fact, the two are diametrically opposed. My biggest challenge when dealing with clients is addressing mindset. When each person enters retirement, he or she has to undergo a mindset change. He or she must change from a growth-and-accumulation mode to an asset-preservation mode when considering financial investments. Part of my expertise includes knowing how to help clients understand the need for that kind of shift.

Over the last ten to twenty years, radical stock-market swings, low investment returns, minimal interest rates, and sagging real-estate values have destroyed the finances of too many retirees and would-be retirees. Sadly, the majority of these people could have protected their hard-earned assets had they only switched their investment mindset before it was too late.

Each person's financial life is divided into three distinct phases: accumulation, preservation, and distribution. These phases are defined by age, income sources, lifestyle needs, and investment approach. In this chapter, we will take an in-depth look into these stages.

## PHASE 1: ACCUMULATION

When we get out of school and enter the workforce, we begin the process of asset accumulation. In this phase, we are earning money to support our current needs and our future needs. This period typically ranges from our twenties until our late fifties or sixties, when we retire. Rather than spending all of our money as it comes in, we should be putting away a chunk of what we earn so it can grow over time into a nice next egg for retirement.

As a brief aside, I realize that if you are reading this book, you are likely past or almost past the accumulation phase. However, maybe you have children or grandchildren who are in or approaching this stage. Many young people do not want to hear about the importance of saving money. Yet they might not know how incredibly important saving is or how much easier it is to save while they are still young and have not already made life decisions that could affect their finances significantly, such as buying a home, having children, going back to school, or switching careers.

**If you start saving 6 percent of your income at age twenty-five and boost your contributions by 1 percent per year until you are contributing 12 percent of your income annually, by the time you are fifty-five you will have saved $500,000 for retirement.** This calculation assumes three factors: that you have a starting salary of $40,000; that you are using a fairly conservative, long-term, portfolio growth rate of 5.5 percent annually; and that your wages will increase by 1.5 percent per year.

I cannot tell you how many people I have met who are in their fifties, sixties, or seventies and who desperately wish they could turn back the clock and follow that advice. If there were one message I could get across to younger folks, it would be this: "Pay yourself first." It is much more important to save a set amount of each paycheck for your future self than it is to spend, spend, and spend on your *present* self.

During the accumulation stage, and particularly on the early side of the stage, you have many more choices about investing than you will in later phases. For example, you can invest in stocks, mutual funds, or commodities, and you can look for riskier investments with potentially higher returns. The downside, of course, is that you may incur possible market losses or even lost principal. Even so, at this point you have a generous amount of time in which you can recoup such losses and respond flexibly to the market's ups and downs.

When you are in this stage, you will find it is much easier to qualify and pay for life insurance and/or long-term-care insurance. In addition to having a longer amount of time to fund the policies amply, you will be protecting yourself and your family throughout your working years in case you suffer unexpected death or injury.

With the exception of insurance policies, almost all of the assets you invest during the accumulation phase are subject to market risk. During this stage, investors typically work with financial advisors who specialize in the growth-and-accumulation mode of investing. That approach is fine as long as you know when to shift the focus from asset *growth* to asset *preservation*.

Think about it. If you are planning to retire, say, in two years, that does not leave you much time to make up for any market losses. Your nest egg will soon be a critical source of income, and your investment mindset must be realigned to keep it safe.

Remember Sandra from Chapter 1? Sandra was seventy-eight when she came to me with $713,000 in assets. At that point, all her money was in high-risk investments. Fortunately, for her, we were able to shift her investments over to safe accounts fairly painlessly, even at a relatively late date. In a perfect world, Sandra would have started that financial transition well before retirement—around age fifty—and her sizable portfolio would not have been touched by the stock market crashes of 2000 or 2008.

## PHASE 1: ACCUMULATION
### AGE 20 TO 60 (APPROXIMATE)

This is the phase of your life to concentrate on the accumulation of assets that will ultimately fund your retirement years. Since you are younger during this phase and have more time to wait out the cyclical nature of the markets, you can afford to take more risks in your choices of investing.

### Experts of Phase 1: Brokers

Most brokers deal in primarily managed money, or investments that require constant monitoring. Although you are at the risk of the stock market, you can achieve the highest return from the types of accounts that most brokers specialize in. Brokers make their money by the continued management of the funds they sell to their clients. Without money to manage, they do not make a fee/commission.

### Phase 1 Investment Vehicles

- Mutual funds, exchange-traded funds, common and preferred stocks, model portfolios
- Asset allocation (diversified portfolios of risk-based investments

## PHASE 2: PRESERVATION

Suppose that for twenty, thirty, or forty years you have been in the accumulation phase, saving and trying to make your savings grow. You may have put some money in riskier investments, which you were able to do because you had time on your side: time for the market to adjust in your favor, or even time to rebuild any lost principal.

Now, you are entering, or have entered, the preservation phase. At this point, what you have saved becomes absolutely critical. Your mindset must shift in importance from the continued accumulation of savings to the preservation and (for most people) the use of those accumulated savings to produce income. Preventing the erosion of the principal and making plans for distribution become priorities.

After years of investing, often aggressively, in risk-type funds, it can be very difficult to taper off the risk and make the transition to treating your funds conservatively. Failing to do so has produced a very real problem that the majority of Americans are facing today: the frightening prospect of running out of money before dying.

Finding an experienced retirement income planner when nearing or entering retirement should be your first move as you make the transition from asset accumulation to asset preservation.

To develop a successful portfolio that will reduce your risk and provide an income plan you cannot outlive, you must find someone who is willing to take money "out of the market." (Brokers and Wall Street advisors make their commissions on money "in the market," so it is not easy to find an individual with this background who will recommend making a change.)

You need someone who knows retirement income planning inside and out, someone who can help you protect your money and keep it in a safe place so you can finance your lifestyle through the remaining years of your life. With your advisor's guidance, you can begin shifting your at-risk money to safe investments guaranteed to provide the income you will need as long as you live.

## PHASE 2: PRESERVATION
### AGE 60 (APPROXIMATE) TO DEATH

During this phase, you should concentrate on preserving the assets you have worked all your life to accumulate. Time is growing shorter, and you now have less time to get back what you could potentially lose. Since timing is so important, you must understand exactly how much risk you can afford to take. Based on your income needs as well as the goals you have set for your hard-earned investment dollars, you must invest accordingly. Keeping your money safe during this phase is a key component to achieving a stable income plant, one that you cannot outlive and can always rely on.

### Experts of Phase 2: Retirement and Estate Planners

Financial professionals who focus their energy on retirees and those soon to be retired deal with investments that preserve assets. Planning for retirement is a tricky business that many investors do not have a sound plan for. Almost 60 percent of retirees run out of money before they run out of life because they did not alter their investment strategies from accumulation to preservation upon entering this phase of life.

### Phase 2 Investment Vehicles

- CDs, insured deposits, government bonds, fixed annuities, fixed index annuities, fixed income models

- True diversification (safe investments with risk tolerance according to individual situations)

## PHASE 3: DISTRIBUTION

In the distribution phase, your assets and legacy are passed on to your beneficiaries and loved ones. Anything you leave behind will then change ownership according to your will and/or trust(s).

While it might seem easy enough to write a will directing how your assets should be divided, it takes better planning than that to complete distribution in the right way for both you and your heirs. At a minimum, this means making sure your estate does not have to go through probate.

All too often, family members and loved ones are forced to deal with a long, drawn-out legal battle in probate court, or with estate attorneys, to settle everything. Would you rather your loved ones have sufficient time to grieve and get back on track with their lives or get caught up in a legal fiasco that could significantly reduce the monetary value of your estate?

Instead of simply worrying about where to invest your money, your advisor also should be determining the best path for protecting your money from loss while minimizing unnecessary taxation and providing the most reliable income possible. By positioning your assets accordingly and developing a failsafe estate plan, your family can avoid probate altogether. (You will learn more about estate planning in Chapter 7.)

You and your retirement income planner should also work closely with an estate lawyer to ensure that your important financial documents are properly executed and updated as needed. This includes your financial power of attorney and health-care directive as well as your will and trust(s).

## PHASE 3: DISTRIBUTION
### *BEYOND DEATH*

This phase determines what happens to the money you have preserved throughout phase 2. Depending on your current financial situation, you may or may not have money left over when your retirement plan has run its course. For those who properly plan to have assets left over for their heirs, it is important to develop a distribution (or "estate") plan for after your death.

Experts of Phase 3: Estate Planning Attorneys and Retirement Planners

The most important financial objective once you have passed away is the distribution of your retirement assets to your heirs in the most efficient and tax-advantageous way possible.

### Phase 3 Investment Vehicles

- Wills, trusts, powers of attorney, etc.
- Avoiding probate and estate tax

## ANOTHER WAY TO LOOK AT IT

The most important thing to remember about the three stages of financial life is that the older we are, the less investment risk we can tolerate. You may have heard of the "Rule of 100," which offers the following advice:

*Take your current age and subtract it from the number 100. The result is the approximate percentage you should not exceed in investments where there is a risk of loss.*

**Example:**

Basis: 100

Less Current Age: minus 58 years

Maximum Amount at Risk: 42 percent

A thirty-year-old individual, for instance, should have roughly 70 percent of his or her funds in stocks and higher-risk assets, with 30 percent reserved for cash and secure income options. Conversely, a seventy-five-year-old individual would have just 25 percent of his or her assets in stocks, with the balance in short-term income. The idea, of course, is that your portfolio should become more conservative as you get older.

## STRUCTURED INCOME PORTFOLIO SYSTEM (SIPS)

As a retirement income specialist, I work primarily with clients who are in the last two stages of their financial lives: asset preservation and distribution. For each of them, I create a structured income portfolio system (SIPS), which is a combination of investments chosen to meet each client's specific income needs throughout the rest of his or her life. Each individual's SIPS is based on the goals and financial information he or she provided during the data intake process discussed in Chapter 2. In formulating the SIPS, I also take inflationary increases and rising out-of-pocket health-care costs into consideration.

A SIPS typically divides a person's assets into three areas: **safe money** for life's necessities, **conservative investments** for extra expenses, and **emergency money** for unexpected situations.

**First, at the core of the SIPS is an insurance contract** through a fixed-income annuity with lifetime income and long-term-care benefits. Although a life-insurance company issues this contract, the contract is not a life-insurance contract; it is an annuity. This setup guarantees a series of contractually bound income payments as long as you and/or your spouse live. This is guaranteed income, even if you live long enough to spend every penny of the money in the contract.

Together, you and I make sure the payments from the insurance contract are enough to cover your income shortfall, which is the amount of money you need beyond your Social Security and pension income to cover ongoing, necessary expenses such as food, shelter, transportation, health care, and so on.

**Next, after covering all of the basic necessities,** we can, if so desired, step out of the completely safe arena and take on a little bit of risk in the markets (I want to put emphasis on "a little bit"). As we discussed earlier in this chapter, as your age increases, your money in the market should decrease. What we are looking for in these conservative investments are solid, dividend-paying equities with forty- or fifty-year histories of paying escalating dividends. (I like to use utilities such as Southern Company and AT&T, or consumer staples such as Coca-Cola and McDonald's.) The money in this area is for your extra expenses, such as buying a new car, taking a vacation, contributing to a grandchild's education, and other things of that nature.

**Finally, the third place we need money is in an emergency fund** with about six months of income that is liquid and easy to access. The emergency fund could be in a money-market, or an interest-bearing, account.

This combination of accounts provides the framework for many a successful retirement plan. There are hundreds of variations; after all, everyone's needs and goals are different. Likewise, there are multitudes of financial instruments you and your retirement income planner can use to help meet your objectives. By applying this basic theory, an experienced retirement income planner can custom-build a plan for you that guarantees you will have the income you need to live comfortably for the rest of your life.

## HEADS UP!

As I said before, at my firm we always factor rising inflation and out-of-pocket health-care costs into our clients' SIPS. In addition to being mindful of these costs, you and your retirement income planner should be aware of some other facts of financial life. Remember, problems seem to bother least those who plan the most.

- ✪ **The surviving spouse:** Surviving spouses are generally at greater risk than they realize of not having enough money after a partner dies. The loss of one Social Security check and some or all of the late spouse's pension income can drastically affect the surviving spouse's standard of living. Taxes may also go up, since filing singly is more expensive than filing jointly. Moreover, in many cases, a significant portion of the family savings has been used for the late spouse's health-care and final expenses. It is important to plan for such contingencies in a couple's retirement income strategy.

- ✪ **Financial considerations of marriage:** Forget the rent-or-buy debate; recent trends reveal that mature adults, age sixty and up, are debating the financial wisdom of getting married or just living together. From 2007 to 2010, the number of adults age sixty or older who were living with an unmarried partner increased by 14 percent. For many, the decision not to marry is more of a financial one than an emotional one. If you are considering tying the knot, you might want to discuss the financial implications with your retirement income planner.

# AGE MATTERS

✪ The three stages of a person's financial life are:

- asset accumulation

- asset preservation

- asset distribution

✪ The "Rule of 100" illustrates how investment risk should decrease as age increases: Subtract your age from 100. The remainder is the maximum percentage of your investment money that can tolerate some market risk. Your age in numerals represents the percentage of your money that should be in safe investments.

✪ The biggest financial problem facing many retirees and preretirees is all in their heads: Their mindset about investing is what causes the issue. All too many people are stuck in the accumulation mode of investing and have difficulty shifting over to a preservation mindset.

✪ People should start making the transition from accumulation mode to preservation mode around age fifty. This often means changing the way they invest; it can also mean changing from a broker or asset accumulation/growth financial advisor to a retirement-income planner who specializes in asset preservation and distribution.

✪ In my practice, we use a structured income portfolio system (SIPS) to assist our clients. Through SIPS, we assemble a set of investments to meet each client's specific income needs throughout the rest of his or her life.

*Chapter 4:*

# TAXES:
# THE BIGGEST
# POTHOLE

PAYING UNNECESSARY TAXES IS THE MOST
COMMON—AND COSTLY—RETIREMENT TRAP.

"Just stop thinking of it as your money, and this'll go a lot easier for both of us."

**M**ost people overpay their income tax. This is just a fact. People do not do this on purpose, of course; they simply do not know any better. They do not know how to take advantage of the rule book that is given to them: the IRS tax code.

As an American citizen, it is your obligation to file your taxes, but it is also your privilege to use that rule book. In other words, you are required to pay your taxes, but not to overpay them.

When I sit down with new clients and go over their tax returns, I find, on average, that they overpaid their taxes for the previous year by at least $3,000. Often, people overpay much more than that. Think back to the couple described in Chapter 2 who were overpaying their taxes by $27,000 each year. Paying more than you need to in taxes is like stumbling over a massive pothole that swallows your money, year after year.

Think about what you could do with that money if it happened to be in your pocket instead of the tax pothole. This money could make a huge difference to your lifestyle in any number of ways. Maybe you would not have to dip into your savings, or perhaps you could treat yourself to a nice vacation. No matter what way you use that money, the key is that the money is *yours* to save or spend, not the government's.

Why are so many people overpaying their taxes? Most often, overpayment is the result of working with a tax *preparer* rather than a tax *planner*. Do you know the difference? It's simple: Tax preparers look at the past, while tax planners look at the future. See if this sounds familiar:

*You gather a lot of information and put it in a big envelope, or a shoebox, or a manila folder, and you go see the person who completes your tax return. He or she says, "Give me a few days. I will get your tax return ready and give you a call."*

*Then that person sits down and goes through all that information you brought over from last year. He or she enters numbers into a computer software program, which in turn figures out your tax return and prints it out.*

*You get a call a few days later, and you go down to the office again. The tax person tells you, "Here you go. This is what you owe Uncle Sam, and this is what you owe me." You write a couple of checks and sign your return, and the person says, "Thanks a lot for your business. I will see you next year."*

That is a tax preparer. Tax preparers are historians. They are working in the past. They are looking at the past and examining the previous year. What can be done about the previous year? Absolutely nothing. It is gone.

A tax planner, in contrast, takes that seven-million-word IRS tax code and applies it to each person's particular situation. There is no cookie-cutter solution. We tax planners apply the rule book to the individual and say, "What can we do today, legally, to keep you from paying too much tax tomorrow?"

In other words, *today* is the day for tax planning. Nothing can be done about this year's returns when this year is gone. What we want to do is find the moves we can make today to preserve your funds in the years to come. For example, how should you hold your assets? How should you take your income? Are you missing deductions? Are there things you can do to lower your future tax liability?

## THE ABSENCE OF TAX PLANNING CREATES OPPORTUNITY COST

What is *opportunity cost*? To define the term, answer these questions: Do you earn interest on an expense? Is the expense (that is, the money spent) accessible? What would the money spent be worth at some future date if you had been able to invest it? The answers to these questions lie in opportunity cost.

I feel so strongly about the importance of coordinating tax planning and investment planning that I go over all my clients' tax returns with my CPA to make sure they are paying as little as possible in taxes. Less tax paid is equivalent to less opportunity cost.

I met with an average, blue-collar, working couple the other day. Since they were holding few assets, I charged them $500 for tax planning and told them, "If I do not save you three times that on your taxes, you do not owe me anything." After I saved them about $5,000 in taxes paid—plus significant opportunity cost—they considered my fee a bargain.

## HOW CAN A ROTH IRA AFFECT YOUR TAXES?

During their working years, most people contribute to a 401(k), an IRA, or a defined contribution plan in order to lay aside money for future retirement income. Uncle Sam allows people to reduce taxable income by the amount of the contribution, thereby lowering retirement contributors' tax obligation each year.

The Roth IRA was established by the Taxpaper Relief Act of 1997 (Public Law 105-34) and named for its chief legislative sponsor, Senator William Roth of Delaware.

The problem for us retirement contributors is that as our funds are invested and grow, so grows our tax obligation to Uncle Sam. Basically, we enter into an agreement lowering our taxes at the time of the contribution, while simultaneously committing to pay them at some point in the future at a tax rate that has yet to be determined. In the future, if taxes increase from what they were when we contributed to the account, we lose. If taxes are lower than when we contributed to the account, we win. Considering our country's looming debt, the likelihood of encountering lower taxes in the future is quite remote.

So what is the payoff for converting a traditional IRA to a Roth IRA, and how is it that you can end up wealthier by paying your tax sooner?

The answer varies depending on your situation. There are several factors involved, including your age, whether you have funds to pay the tax outside your IRA, and whether you need income from your account to live on.

A Roth IRA can offer you more funds than a traditional IRA that has the same balance. Suppose you have a Roth IRA with a $100,000 balance. If you meet all the rules of holding an IRA, you will not pay tax when you withdraw that $100,000 and all the earnings it generates.

Compare a traditional IRA with the same balance. When you withdraw that $100,000, you will pay a fraction of that amount to the IRS. You will also hand over a fraction of all your earnings on that $100,000. The IRS actually partly owns and is a partner in your IRA. The more your IRA investment makes, the larger the share your IRS partner owns.

The size of the fraction your IRS partner owns depends on your tax bracket. The higher your tax bracket during the period in which you make withdrawals, the smaller your share of the IRA. If your federal tax bracket is 33 percent, for instance, a Roth IRA is effectively 50 percent larger than a traditional IRA with the same balance.

Another benefit of a Roth IRA is that you do not have to take *required minimum distributions*, or RMDs, as you would with a traditional IRA. When you are seventy-and-one-half years old, your IRS partner requires you to start taking RMDs, which are withdrawals, from your IRA. If you do not need these distributions to live on, and the ultimate purpose of your IRA is security for your spouse after you are gone or to leave as a legacy to your heirs, these distributions and the tax you pay are defeating your goal. If you have a Roth IRA, you avoid RMDs, which can produce huge tax savings and permit you to accumulate much greater wealth in your later years.

The minimum distribution rules do not apply to a Roth IRA until after the owner dies. As a result of this rule, a Roth IRA owner who survives well past seventy-and-one-half may leave a much greater amount of wealth to a spouse, children, or other beneficiaries. For this reason, moving IRA funds to a Roth IRA can pay off handsomely.

If you have enough wealth to be concerned about estate tax, you should consider another benefit of a Roth IRA conversion. The estate tax applies to your total assets at death, including assets held in a traditional IRA or a Roth IRA. The difference is that the estate tax does not notice that the Roth IRA offers its holder a larger amount of money from which to draw. As a result, the amount of estate tax on a $500,000 IRA is the same whether it is a traditional IRA or a Roth IRA.

Consider how this plays out for your beneficiaries. If they inherit a traditional IRA, they will have to pay income tax on the amounts they withdraw. The value of what you transfer to them is reduced by the amount of the taxes. In contrast, if they receive a Roth IRA, they get to keep the amounts they withdraw.

What using a Roth IRA boils down to is that you are reducing the size of your estate—by prepaying the tax on your IRA—without reducing the value of your estate. Today, most people do not have enough wealth to be concerned with estate tax, but no one can be sure of what Congress will do in the future with the debt or the unfunded promises the government has made.

The next financial advantage of converting to a Roth IRA is shifting rates. The idea is to pay tax when your rates are low rather than high. Toward that end, it would probably be a smart thing to convert as much of your traditional IRA to a Roth IRA as you can without jumping to the next tax bracket.

While we do not know what the future holds, I want to bring a few numbers to your attention. Visit the website www.usdebtclock.org. When you bring up the site, you will see that the debt of the U.S. government is $16 trillion. Look at the bottom of the site's home page, toward the middle, and you will see another astonishing number. This number is $121 trillion, which is approximately 7.5 times the national debt. This number is the amount in unfunded liabilities, or promises the government has made, for which the government does not have the money to pay. This number comes from promises made through Social Security, prescription drugs, and Medicare. It is my judgment that regardless of the political party in power, regardless of the president, and regardless of what you are being told, taxes must increase and spending must decrease. Get ready for the services you receive from the government to decrease, and get ready to pay more for what you do get.

Traditional IRA or Roth IRA? That is the question; you must decide.

## COMMON TAX OVERSIGHTS

The most common mistake I find on clients' returns is that they have been **paying taxes on interest earned but not spent.** Take a look at your tax return. Any amount of income shown on lines 7 and 21 is taxable income. If you have income showing on lines 8a, 9a, or 13, and you do not need that income to live on, you are overpaying your taxes and experiencing opportunity cost. Depending on your particular situation, there are many other areas in which you could be overpaying your income tax. In the following paragraphs, I will give you a few examples.

**Business owners not taking the deductions for which they are eligible:** From experience, I would say business owners and medical professionals overpay their taxes the most. I once had a physician tell me that in medical school he learned a skill that rewarded him with a nice income. Unfortunately, no one in medical school had taught him what to do with that income. The fact is, business owners are very busy running the businesses and can let things slip through the cracks, causing overpayment of taxes. Business owners have great opportunities to pay fewer taxes through proper tax planning. If your income is uncommon, shouldn't you be using uncommon techniques to save on taxes?

**Forgetting to take or miscalculating required minimum distributions (RMDs):** As previously noted, when you turn seventy-and-one-half, the IRS requires that you begin taking distributions from your qualified accounts, such as IRA, 401(k), 403(b), and SEP accounts. All of your working life, Uncle Sam has allowed you to lay aside money in a qualified retirement account and defer the taxes. Then, when you turn seventy-and-one-half, Uncle Sam figures it is time to start settling up on the taxes he did not collect throughout your working life.

You can estimate your own RMD by looking up your life expectancy and dividing your year-end IRA balance by the number of years of your life expectancy, or the number representing the joint life expectancy for you and a spouse. Use the tables given in Appendix C of IRS Publication 590, Individual Retirement Arrangements.

If you fail to take out an RMD, the IRS will charge you a penalty of 50 percent of the RMD you were supposed to take. You may wish to spend down your traditional IRA and 401(k) assets first, and then spend down nontaxable sources of income, such as Roth IRAs and life-insurance cash values. You may also wish to divide your income between taxable and nontaxable sources so that your taxable income does not push you into a higher tax bracket. This is the planning technique of *tax diversification.*

**Forgetting to plan for taxes on your Social Security income:** At some points, you may have to pay federal income taxes on Social Security benefits. This usually happens only if you have other income, such as wages, self-employment, interest, dividends, or other taxable income that must be reported on your tax return. The amount of your Social Security income, plus income from any of these other sources, is considered your *combined income.*

Based on Internal Revenue Service rules, no one pays federal income tax on more than 85 percent of his or her Social Security benefits.

✪ **If you file a federal tax return as an individual,** and your combined income is between $25,000 and $34,000, you may have to pay income tax on up to 50 percent of your Social Security benefits.

- ▫ If your combined income is more than $34,000, up to 85 percent of your benefits may be taxable.

- ✪ **If you file a joint return,** and you and your spouse have a combined income that is between $32,000 and $44,000, you may have to pay income tax on up to 50 percent of your benefits.

  - ▫ If your combined income is more than $44,000, up to 85 percent of your benefits may be taxable.

- ✪ If you are married and file a separate tax return, you probably will pay taxes on your benefits.

## HOW LONG SHOULD YOU MAINTAIN FINANCIAL DOCUMENTS?

The IRS has three years from the date of a tax return to assess additional tax if all income was reported correctly. However, the IRS requires that you be able to produce return documentation for up to six years if you did not report income that made up more than 25 percent of the gross income you did report on a particular return. Furthermore, there is no statute of limitations for tax fraud or failure to file a return altogether.

The following is a guide for retaining financial records:

- household bills: one month, unless used as documentation for tax purposes

- credit card statements: one month

- investment account statements: six years

- tax returns/support documentation: minimum of six years

- trusts, deeds, vehicle titles: indefinitely

- medical history details: indefinitely

- Social Security/pension statements: indefinitely

# TAXES: THE BIGGEST POTHOLE

✪ When I sit down with new clients and go over their tax returns, I find, on average, that they have overpaid their taxes for the previous year by at least $3,000. Often, they have overpaid much more than that.

✪ Tax preparing and tax planning are two very different things. Tax preparing looks at the past; tax planning looks at the future. Make sure you are getting the tax planning help you need to steer clear of potential tax potholes that can cost you thousands of dollars each year.

✪ I feel so strongly about the importance of coordinating tax planning and investment planning that I go over all my clients' tax returns with my CPA to make sure my clients are paying as little as possible in taxes.

✪ Depending on a person's overall financial situation, it may be tax-advantageous to convert assets from a traditional IRA to a Roth IRA.

✪ The most common tax mistakes I see retirees make are:

- paying tax on interest income earned but not spent

- not taking the deductions for which they are eligible (this applies to business owners particularly)

- forgetting to take or miscalculating required minimum distributions (RMDS)

- forgetting to plan for taxes on Social Security income

*Chapter 5:*

# GET THE MOST MILEAGE FROM YOUR MONEY

## FACTORS AFFECTING SOCIAL SECURITY

The biggest story in Social Security today concerns the large number of baby boomers set to retire over the next 20 years and the relatively smaller younger generations feeding Social Security payroll taxes into the system. On average, today's seniors are living longer than any previous generation. While that's good news, it also presents several new challenges. A longer life increases the likelihood that you'll have increased medical and long-term care expenses throughout much of your retirement. This is particularly true if you've been active all of your life – as many of today's baby boomers have been.

Furthermore, the value of your nest egg could be more significantly impacted by increases in the cost of living over a longer term. And, quite simply, you could outlive your savings. When you consider all of these factors, it is important to make informed decisions about when to begin receiving Social Security benefits within the context of your overall retirement income strategy.

Other sources of retirement income, such as pension plans, 401(k) plans, IRAs, annuities, tax-exempt and taxable securities should be carefully evaluated in light of various factors. For example, generating a reliable fixed income versus variable, at-risk income.

Social Security benefits are largely funded by today's workers via payroll taxes. In 2011, the Old-Age and Survivors Insurance and Disability Insurance Trust Funds collected $805.1 billion in revenues from the following sources:

- 82.8% from payroll taxes and reimbursements from the General Fund of the Treasury

- 3.0% from income taxes on Social Security benefits

- 14.2% from interest earned on the government bonds held by the trust funds

The number of retired workers is projected to double in less than 30 years. Adding to the Social Security funding dilemma, people are also living longer and the national birth rate is low. As a result, the ratio of workers paying Social Security taxes to people collecting benefits is projected to fall from 2.9 to 1 in 2011 to 2.0 to 1 in 2034.

The Trustees Report projects that there will be a shortfall in payroll taxes needed to fund benefits, yet the redemption of trust fund assets will be sufficient to allow for full payment of scheduled benefits until 2032. At that point, payroll taxes and other income will be sufficient to pay only 75% of program costs.

As of 2013, full retirement age (referred to as FRA) is age 66 for anyone born in 1943 or later. If you were born between 1943 and 1962, full retirement age is 66 plus 2-month increments depending on the month of your birthday. If you were born in 1960 or later, full retirement age is 67. You may begin taking benefits starting at age 62, but they will be permanently reduced. Covered workers need 40 credits to be eligible for their own benefit, which works out to about 10 years of work history. Your benefit is calculated based on your average earnings over the highest-earning 35 years.

## FULL RETIREMENT AND AGE 62 BENEFIT
### *(By Year of Birth)*

| Year of Birth [1] | Full (normal) Retirement Age | Months between age 62 and full retirement age [2] | At Age 62 [3] | | | |
|---|---|---|---|---|---|---|
| | | | A $1000 retirement benefit would be reduced to | The retirement benefit is reduced by [4] | A $500 spouse's benefit would be reduced to | The spouse's benefit is reduced by [5] |
| 1937 or earlier | 65 | 36 | $800 | 20.00% | $375 | 25.00% |
| 1938 | 65 and 2 months | 38 | $791 | 20.83% | $370 | 25.83% |
| 1939 | 65 and 4 months | 40 | $783 | 21.67% | $366 | 26.67% |
| 1940 | 65 and 6 months | 42 | $775 | 22.50% | $362 | 27.50% |
| 1941 | 65 and 8 months | 44 | $766 | 23.33% | $358 | 28.33% |
| 1942 | 65 and 10 months | 46 | $758 | 24.17% | $354 | 29.17% |
| 1943-1954 | 66 | 48 | $750 | 25.00% | $350 | 30.00% |
| 1955 | 66 and 2 months | 50 | $741 | 25.83% | $345 | 30.83% |
| 1956 | 66 and 4 months | 52 | $733 | 26.67% | $341 | 31.67% |
| 1957 | 66 and 6 months | 54 | $725 | 27.50% | $337 | 32.50% |
| 1958 | 66 and 8 months | 56 | $716 | 28.33% | $333 | 33.33% |
| 1959 | 66 and 10 months | 58 | $708 | 29.17% | $329 | 34.17% |
| 1960 and later | 67 | 60 | $700 | 30.00% | $325 | 35.00% |

*Social Security Administration, http://www.socialsecurity.gov/retire2/agereduction.htm, retrieved January 8, 2013.*

Working up to full retirement age may increase your benefit while at the same time any contributions you continue to make to a 401(k) plan and/or investment portfolio will have more time to potentially accrue higher gains.

No matter what age you begin receiving Social Security benefits, your payout will receive an automatic annual cost of living adjustment when there is a comparative increase in the consumer price index.

Common sense may tell you that – among couples – the higher earner should claim benefits as early as possible and the lower earner should delay in order to receive a higher benefit. In reality, the exact opposite may be the better option because if the higher earner claims early and then dies first, he or she is likely to have shortchanged the lower earner's survivor benefit.

In this scenario, the higher earner should delay claiming benefits so that the lower earner can claim the highest possible benefit for life – whether it's the lower earner's own benefit or a derivative of the higher-earner's highest available benefit. If the lower earner dies first there is no lost benefit, as the higher earner simply keeps his or her own benefit.

Spousal or "derivative" Social Security benefits are determined by each of their work history and earnings, and the age at which they apply for and/or begin drawing benefits.

When women take time off the workforce to have children, raise children, or even provide care for senior parents, years with part-time or zero earnings may factor into the 35 years and result in a much lower benefit than people who work fulltime throughout their adult lives. This is why many women might qualify for a higher benefit based on their husband's work history.

The spousal – or derivative – benefit is 50% of the higher earner's accrued benefit at the spouse's full retirement age. Should the higher-earning spouse start taking benefits earlier than full retirement age, the spouse's derivative benefit will be less.

In order for the lower-earning spouse to collect benefits based on the higher earner's history, the higher earner must apply for Social Security retirement benefits first. However, if the higher-earning spouse has reached full retirement age, he or she may apply for benefits and then file to suspend drawing benefits until later. This enables the higher-earner to accrue a higher benefit via more earnings contributions and Delayed Retirement Credits.

If you do not feel the need to draw benefits at full retirement age and/or would like to continue working, you are eligible to earn Delayed Retirement Credits (DRC) on your future benefits for each full year that you do not start receiving benefits after you've reached full retirement age.

- ✪ Currently the Delayed Retirement Credit is 8% per year for those born in 1943 or later

- ✪ The credit stops once you reach age 70

- ✪ A spouse may draw benefits while the higher earner accrues Delayed Benefit Credits

- ✪ Derivative benefits for your spouse do not include any <u>Delayed Retirement Credits</u>

If you are married and have reached full retirement age, you have a couple of options. You may claim benefits either on your work history or your spouse's. Or, you can draw the spousal benefit and allow your own benefit to accrue Delayed Retirement Credits until you turn age 70. At that point you can apply for your own work history benefit and switch over to yours (assuming it is higher than the derivative amount).

Here is an example of how it works:

- ✪ Ed and Sarah both turn age 66 (full retirement age)

- ✪ Ed's monthly benefit is $1,400; Sarah's is $1,000

- ✪ Ed files for benefits and Sarah begins drawing her spousal benefit (50% of Ed's = $700)

- ✪ Sarah continues working and earning towards her own benefits, while also earning Delayed Retirement Credits

- ✪ At age 70, Sarah applies for her own benefit based on her work history, which is now $1,370 a month

- ✪ Her payout automatically switches to the higher benefit amount.

Once you reach full retirement age, you may apply for a restricted benefit based on your spouses' earnings as long as that earner is already receiving benefits. Even if you are the higher earner, you may instruct Social Security to restrict your benefit to your spouses' earnings – which means you will be entitled to up to 50% of the benefit your spouse is receiving. This strategy enables you to earn Delayed Retirement Credits up until age 70, at which time you can switch to your own benefit. This option is not available prior to full retirement age.

If a couple was married for at least 10 years and then divorces, either one of the spouses may qualify for Social Security benefits at age 62 under the other's work history. Even if the higher-earning ex has not applied for benefits yet, as long as he is eligible for them and the couple has been divorced for at least two years, the other ex may apply for a derivative benefit. Once an ex-spouse remarries an opposite sex spouse, he or she is no longer eligible to receive a benefit based on the first spouse's work history unless the second (third, forth, etc.) marriage ends in divorce, annulment or death. You are eligible for the highest derivative available from any number of ex-spouses as long as each marriage lasted at least 10 years and you are not currently married.

Among married couples, the age at which the higher-earning spouse applies for Social Security benefits is very important, since the surviving spouse is entitled to the higher of his or her own or the deceased spouse's benefit. The higher earner can increase the survivor's benefit by waiting to receive any benefits until age 70. If the higher-earning spouse dies, the widow(er) is entitled to the higher earner's full retirement benefit and may begin receiving benefits starting at age 60 (or at any age if he or she has a child under age 16 or disabled). Should the widow(er) remarry, the Social Security benefit for the widow(er) will terminate – but the benefit for the eligible child will not.

A surviving spouse may also claim a reduced benefit on the deceased's working record and then switch to his or her own later. The surviving spouse may wait until full retirement age to accrue a higher benefit, or even delay benefits until age 70 to accrue Delayed Retirement Credits based on his or her own work history. Once the survivor applies for his/her own benefit, the payout will automatically be at the highest amount.

Once you reach full retirement age, there is no longer an earnings limit – meaning you can earn any amount of income without it impacting your benefits.

**Loss of Social Security retirement benefits:**

In years prior to full retirement age, $1 in benefits will be lost for every $2 of earnings in excess of $15,120. In the year of full retirement age, $1 in benefits will be lost for every $3 of earnings in excess of $40,080 (applies only to months of earnings prior to full retirement age). There is no limit on earnings beginning the month an individual attains full retirement age.

According to the 2011 Risk and Process of Retirement Survey by the Society of Actuaries, only 35% of Americans aged 45 to 80 report that they have a detailed retirement income plan designed to manage the risk of running short of money. To help you prepare for a possible reduction in Social Security benefits and/or an overall shortfall in your retirement income, calculate the general amount of income you expect to need in retirement.

Add up your monthly expenses and factor in a 3.23% long-term annual inflation rate (the average annual inflation rate from 1913 through 2012). If the retirement age increases in the future, you may be able to continue working and delay your own retirement. However, if you can't and need to retire before the full retirement age, you'll need to factor in the potential for reduced Social Security benefits during those years.

You may receive a personalized estimate of your Social Security benefits by using the online Retirement Estimator at http://ssa.gov/estimator.

Once you've identified your level of benefits, subtract this amount from the total income you've calculated that you need. The balance will give you an idea of the amount that could need to come from other sources.

One way to supplement your Social Security benefits is to save and invest as much as you can now toward your retirement. Other ideas including maximizing your contributions to an employer plan, such as a 401(k) or 403(b) or contribute whatever you can to a Roth or traditional IRA.

If you are not eligible for a tax deduction on IRA contributions due to your participation in an employer retirement plan, you may want to consider contributing to a Roth as well, so you can benefit from tax-free distributions in retirement.

**2013 Contributions:**

- ✪ Participants in employer-sponsored retirement plans, such as 401(k)s, 403(b)s, 457s or Thrift Savings Plans may contribute up to $17,500 in 2013 ($23,000 for employees 50 or older)

- ✪ 2013 annual limit for all IRAs combined is $5,500 ($6,500 for age 50+)

The simple fact is that Social Security may not always be straightforward. Just like every other facet of retirement planning, there are strategies you can employ to optimize the benefits you are eligible to receive – particularly among married couples.

Many people are hesitant to delay receiving benefits because they don't want to lose money they've contributed to the system for the last 35 years. While people who apply for Social Security benefits early will get more dollars if they die soon after, the opposite is also true – they will receive less if they live significantly longer.

The monthly benefit paid out at age 62 is actuarially reduced to account for the eight more years that the recipient will be paid benefits as compared to someone who begins drawing payouts at age 70. Furthermore, the person who waits to claim benefits at age 70 will receive 76% more (real) dollars per month for the rest of his life than if he claimed benefits at age 62.

What's most important in making Social Security decisions for your situation is at what point you can no longer live comfortably without those benefits due to job loss, health care expenses or other issues. The question isn't how to beat the system, but rather how to optimize the amount of income you receive for the length of time that you need it.

For this reason, it's important to consult with a financial professional experienced in Social Security distributions to review different payout scenarios to help determine the optimal time to file and when to actually begin drawing your benefits.

> Undisclosed fees and bad advice are holes in your
> financial gas tank just waiting to be fixed.

There is a huge amount of money continuously going through Wall Street. Look at those people in their $2,000 suits and their chauffeured limousines, and it does not take long to realize that a great deal of the money that the average guy is investing in his 401(k) or brokerage account is sticking to somebody else's hands as it passes through them.

I think of this as Wall Street's big dirty secret. This secret is kind of like an iceberg. People say that when you see an iceberg, you are only looking at 10 percent of it; 90 percent is hidden beneath the water. That disparate ratio is similar to the ways in which expense ratios, advisory fees, operating fees, and hidden expenses are lurking in your investments.

When people initially come in to meet me and I am going over their finances, I will ask them, "What are you paying for your investments?"

Some people will be honest and say, "I do not know," while others will say, "Oh, a half percent," or, "My advisor tells me I am paying such-and-such percent." When I dissect and analyze the investments they own, I often find those fees are much, much higher.

I will give you an example. A couple, the Whitneys, came in and visited with me. They had about $500,000 in an investment account, which was basically in mutual funds. Their mutual fund's annual report reported that their yearly expenses were around 1.25 percent. When I got in to the account and studied what they were holding, I found that the Whitneys' actual fees were 2.92 percent. On a $563,000 portfolio, they were paying $16,458 a year in fees. That is a great deal of money. Over ten years, the amount they were paying in fees became worth more than a quarter of their entire portfolio. That is just not right.

Think of it this way: The first time you played tic-tac-toe, you

Assume that you are an employee with thirty-five years until retirement and a current 401(k) account balance of $25,000. If returns on investments in your account over the next thirty-five years average 7 percent and fees and expenses reduce your average returns by 0.5 percent, your account balance will grow to $227,000 at retirement, even if there are no further contributions to your account. If fees and expenses are 1.5 percent, however, your account balance will grow to only $163,000. The difference of 1 percent in fees and expenses would reduce your account balance at retirement by 28 percent.

probably lost because you were playing with someone who knew the rules of the game, and you did not. This scenario is similar to how things go on Wall Street. Wall Street brokers know the rules of the game, and they are going to win every time.

In those mutual fund annual reports you get in the mail, you will find information about A shares, B shares, C shares, and so on. Does anyone ever explain that if you buy an A share, you are paying an up-front commission to the person who sold it to you? Normally, that commission is about 5.75 percent. Suppose you bought $10,000 worth of a mutual fund. You did not get $10,000 worth because you paid a 5.75 percent up-front sales cost. You only got $9,425 worth, since you paid $575, as a commission, to the broker or advisor who sold the fund to you. That same broker or advisor will continue to make a commission on an annual basis.

If you wish to deal in assets that involve risk, you cannot escape fees. These fees also become more difficult to uncover. Unfortunately, investing in securities often carries both disclosed and undisclosed fees and commissions. However, by understanding what you are paying now, you will have a better idea of the type of value you are receiving. Let's dive into some of the more common risk-type investments so I can show you what you are really paying to own each investment.

## MUTUAL FUNDS

Mutual funds may be the most common risk-type investment. They might also be the most expensive. The most common cost in a mutual fund is the expense ratio, or the standard measure of how costly a fund is to own. In fact, according to Morningstar, the average expense ratio is estimated at 1.31 percent. These costs are paid to the portfolio manager.

However, it is the undisclosed costs that can make a mutual fund two to three times more expensive than its advertised expense ratio. Mutual funds also have *brokerage commissions, bid-ask spreads,* opportunity costs (discussed earlier), and *market-impact costs. Brokerage commissions* are paid to the firm that sells you the securities. *Bid-ask spreads* estimate the gap between the lowest price someone is willing to pay for said security and the highest price. *Market-impact costs* are often as much as one-and-one-half times the amount of the brokerage commissions.

As if mutual funds were not difficult enough to understand, they come with what is known as a *prospectus*. A *prospectus* is usually a long-winded document that explains in great detail the investment objectives, level of risk, costs and fees, past fund performance, fund management objectives, and so on. Prospectuses are written by attorneys, filled with difficult-to-understand legal jargon, and largely overlooked by the average investor.

Make sure you understand whether or not your mutual funds are back-end loaded or front-end loaded. Many mutual funds will have a load attached to the purchase (front end) or the sale (back end) of the fund. This load is paid to the broker-dealer, which means that you immediately start in a deficit. You can find no-load funds that are usually much better options than funds that have sales loads.

Commissionable mutual funds are also separated by *share class*. There are four main types of commissionable mutual fund classes, and I will discuss each below.

- ✪ *Class A shares* carry lower *12b-1* (that is, operational) fees and usually require a larger initial investment. Many A shares also have front-end loads that subtract a fee from your initial investment. The commissions usually get smaller as the investment gets larger.

- ✪ *Class B shares* are classified by the back-end load with which they come. Therefore, they do not have front-end loads. This means your entire initial investment earns interest. Their yearly expense ratio is higher than that of Class A shares.

- ✪ *Class C shares* are classified as *level-loaded* funds. They have the highest expense ratios of all three classes, carry back-end loads, and offer no opportunity to convert to a different share class.

- ✪ *No-load funds* are sold without a commission or sales charge. The main reason they do not have a charge is because these shares are distributed directly by the investment company rather than a secondary party.

Annual account fees or custodial fees can also come into play. Depending on the size of the overall fund, a management fee may apply. This is the cost your broker is charging you—in addition to everything else listed—to "manage" your mutual fund portfolio.


## VARIABLE ANNUITIES

*Variable annuities* are considered risk-type assets because the value of the annuity goes up and down with the value of the funds it holds. A variable annuity is one of the most expensive places you can park your dollars. Brokers and bankers love to sell these fee-loaded accounts.

Variable annuities are made up of subaccounts holding various mutual funds and the stock and bond funds within those mutual funds. They also carry insurance-related costs, including mortality and risk charges as well as administrative and fund expenses. In fact, variable annuities' fees can total as much as 3 percent a year or more.

## BROKER OR FIDUCIARY?

Typically, brokers are paid through commissions, which can certainly complicate clients' relationships with them. They work according to what is called a *suitability standard*, which means they need only find you a product that is suitable for your situation.

What does that mean, exactly?

Let's say we have got three different mutual funds, or three different investment products, and all three are suitable for your investment needs. Each of the three products has a different commission. Since the broker works on a commission structure, human nature is probably going to dictate that he or she will bring to you the one that pays the highest commission.

Brokerage firms also earn fees from investment companies for promoting their products, which is known as *pay to play*. Here is how that works: Suppose I start up "Don's Mutual Fund," and you are an investment advisor. I say to you, "Hey, I've started up a mutual fund, and I'd like you to help me to get some money in it. Here's what I will do for you. If you help me get money in this fund, I will kick such-and-such amount back to you."

Brokerage firms earn money in that fashion. Not only do they earn money by charging their clients fees, but they also earn money in a secondary way, since the funds that they sell the client kick money back to them. A broker is free to recommend whichever products compensate the broker more generously, rather than what might be best for the investor.

What is best for the investor? It is best for an investor to deal with a fiduciary, an advisor who is required by law to place clients' best interests before his or her own. As a fiduciary, you must find the best product available for your clients' needs by law; moreover, you must work in your clients' best interest, not just in finding investments that are suitable for their needs.

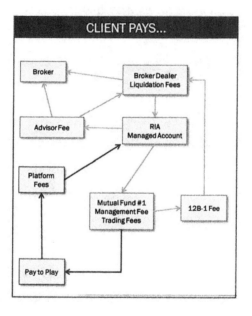

The first chart (above) illustrates the brokerage or retail investment world. As a client in that world, your money passes through many hands, and each time it passes, a little of it sticks to the hands of the person who is touching it. Studies show that over a lifetime of investing, virtually half your investment returns can be taken from you in fees and charges.

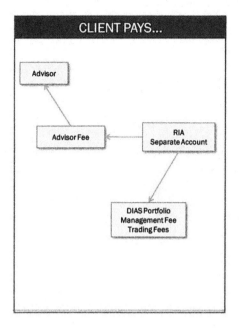

The second chart shows the world of the institutional investor who owns a separate account and works with a fiduciary. As you can see, as an investor working with a fiduciary, and investing in a dynamic investment allocation strategy (DIAS) more of your money stays in your account. The reason? Institutional investing versus retail investing, lower investment cost.

Remember, fiduciaries are bound by law to do what is best for the client. Fiduciaries, including myself, do not work on commission; we try to grow our clients' portfolios as much as we can because that is how we make money. We charge clients a fee based on the value of their portfolios. We do not charge commissions or receive

Fiduciaries are *registered investment advisors* (RIAs), as opposed to *broker-dealer representatives.*

kickbacks. Instead, we provide the best possible guidance and meet each client's needs.

## PIECEMEAL ADVICE, OR ANOTHER HOLE IN THE TANK

Many people work with several professionals who handle various aspects of their money and investments. For example, a single person might have a CPA to file tax returns; a banker to purchase CDs; a broker to buy stocks, bonds, or mutual funds; an insurance agent to purchase life insurance; and an attorney to draft a will and/or trust(s).

Is anyone coordinating who is doing what? Probably not. Remember, in the last chapter, I told you that I review each of my client's tax returns with my CPA to make sure the clients are paying as little in taxes as possible. Unless your money people are working together in a similar manner, you are not getting the most mileage for your money.

Yes, an attorney must draft your estate-related documents. That does not necessarily mean he or she knows what type of trust is best for your financial situation. Likewise, an insurance agent will be more than happy to sell you an insurance policy, but he or she may now know whether it is the best one for your particular needs.

Working with multiple people on the finance-related aspects of your life is probably better than working with no one—probably. I cannot tell you how many times I have gone through clients' financial documentation and found huge tax overpayments, investments that virtually cancel each other out, powerless powers of attorney, and other oversights that are costing people dearly.

I am not saying these professionals are maliciously giving bad advice. On the contrary, they may believe they are giving good advice. Yet there is only so much any advisor can do when working in a vacuum. That is why I take an integrated approach to my clients' retirement planning. My practice includes income and investment planning, as well as tax advisory and estate-planning services; in fact, I am a board-certified estate planner.

Finding a practice that uses a similar big-picture model will bring you the peace of mind that comes with knowing all the pieces of your retirement plan are working together for your maximum benefit, not unlike a perfectly tuned engine ready to power the smoothest and most efficient retirement drive possible.

## THREE REASONS TO ROLL 401(K) ASSETS INTO AN IRA

Many people who change employers or retire choose to leave their accumulated assets in the former employer's 401(k) plan. Actually, they do not always make a conscious choice to do so; they may have other priorities to deal with and may not understand or have time to explore other options or the advantages of doing so.

The reality is that the greatest advantage of 401(k) retirement plans is the employer's matching to the account. Once you leave an employer, that advantage ends. From then onward, your money will accumulate only if your investment choices perform well.

You should be aware of the benefits of your newfound freedom regarding these assets. You have the option to roll them into another tax-deferred account and invest in just about any type of investment—or variety of investments—using an IRA.

### IRA Options

The simplest way to conduct a rollover is to a traditional IRA, wherein your assets may continue to grow tax-deferred, and you have more options to diversify your investment choices. You also have the option to transfer your assets to a Roth IRA. In this scenario, you would have to pay income taxes on the full amount rolled over (even if a portion is, technically, gains). However, after that, any accumulated earnings would be available tax-free during retirement (assuming you withdraw them after age fifty-nine-and-one-half).

The taxes you pay on a Roth rollover may take a significant chunk out of your earnings. However, if you have a reasonably long investment time frame (ten years or more) ahead, you may benefit from tax-advantaged growth and tax-free distributions. Note that if you pay taxes on a Roth IRA rollover with your 401(k) account proceeds, that money is deemed a distribution and will be subject to taxes and any applicable penalties.

**Reasons to Roll**

*Lower Fees and Expenses*

Employer-sponsored plans have made the news recently due to new requirements for transparency regarding the fees charged by administrators. These fees are among the industry's highest account and management fees. One of the reasons funds or investments within a retirement plan are accompanied by higher fees is because they are considered special purpose funds and may not have the asset size of comparable, publicly available investment options. In contrast, the average IRA custodian, either direct or via an advisor, charges no annual administrative fee. You can earn potentially thousands of dollars more by rolling over employer plan assets based on fees alone.

For example, take the hypothetical case of a thirty-year-old employee who has accumulated a $30,000 balance in his 401(k) and plans to retire at age sixty-five. Let's assume he earns an average annual return of 7 percent, regardless of whether he maintains the 401(k) or rolls over the plan to an IRA. However, his 401(k) plan has an annual fund expense ratio of 0.7 percent and an annual administrative fee of 0.5 percent; in contrast, the IRA has an average annual fund expense ratio of only 0.4 percent. By the time he turns sixty-five, his IRA account would return approximately $65,000 more than his 401(k) account.

Keep in mind that if you like the investments you have selected in your 401(k) plan, there is a good chance you can replicate those same choices and allocations in an IRA rollover account. In this scenario, you could build substantially more wealth over time while investing in the exact same holdings, simply by reducing your fees.

*Increased Investment Options*
If you would like to open up your retirement assets to a larger selection of investments, rolling your plan directly to a qualified IRA gives you access to more than 15,000 mutual funds and 1,000 exchange-traded funds (ETFs) on the market, all of which are available through most advisors or fund supermarkets. You also have the option of investing in any stock, bond, or tradable security through your IRA account.

*Better Advice*
By working with an advisor of your choice, you will receive much more individualized advice tailored directly to your needs and your tolerance for risk; this advice should include an allocation that works in concert with your overall portfolio and financial picture.

...........................................................................................

[END OF CHAPTER WRAP-UP]

# GET THE MOST MILEAGE FOR YOUR MONEY

✪ The way you draw Social Security in retirement can mean as much as $100,000 in additional income. See an experienced financial professional to maximize Social Security.

✪ Most people have no idea how much their investments are costing them in disclosed and undisclosed fees. Broker, mutual fund, 401(k), operational, custodial, and management fees can eat up a sizable portion of your investment returns.

✪ Mutual funds and variable annuities are two of the most fee-laden investment types. You need to be aware of how much you are paying in fees on these accounts and how much money in fees is going into your broker's pocket.

✪ When choosing a financial professional, make sure he or she is a fiduciary. Fiduciaries are bound by law to provide the very best financial advice of which they are capable. They are required to put their clients' interests ahead of their own. Financial advisors or brokers who are not fiduciaries are only required to provide sound financial advice. It may not be the best financial advice for the client's situation, and it very well might be more lucrative for the advisor than the client.

✪ Even the smartest, most successful people need help developing and implementing failsafe retirement plans. The best plans integrate:

- income planning

- investment planning

- tax planning

- health-care planning

- estate planning

Only when these pieces are developed collectively can you make sure your money is working as hard for you as you worked for it.

*Chapter 6:*

# PREPARE FOR A LONG-TERM DETOUR

LONG-TERM HEALTH CARE IS AN EXPENSIVE AND NECESSARY REALITY FOR MOST RETIREES. PLAN FOR IT, OR YOUR RETIREMENT JOURNEY MAY TAKE AN ABRUPT TURN FOR THE WORSE.

As much as we all hate to admit it, there will come a time when it is likely that we will need assistance in performing even some of life's most basic activities. It is actually easier for many people to come to grips with their own mortality, or death, than it is for them to imagine being in a state of declining fragility and needing help with even the simplest tasks.

Our stubborn attempts to deny that this need will arise in us does not alter the fact that **70 percent of Americans who reach retirement age will at some point need long-term-care services.** With the cost of nursing homes at about $7,000 a month (in today's dollars and rising at about 5 percent annually), assisted-living facilities at approximately $3,500 a month, and in-home services at a minimum of $2,500 a month, it is no mystery why long-term care is the number-one reason for impoverishment among the elderly.

- On average, someone who is 65 today will need some type of long-term-care services and support for 3 years.

- Women need care longer (on average 3.7 years) than men (on average 2.2 years), mostly because women usually live longer.

- While about one-third of today's 65-year-olds may never need long-term-care service and support, 20 percent will need care for longer than 5 years.

The problem is that people are largely uninformed and unrealistic about long-term care. When I sit down and talk with clients about retirement planning and long-term care, I will often hear something like, "My daughter said she would not let me go to a nursing home," or "My wife will take care of me."

The reality is, your children will probably be working and saving for their own retirement. Their work schedules and other family responsibilities will demand most of their time. As for your spouse, it is very likely that he or she may also need care. No matter how much someone loves you, you cannot expect him or her to drop everything he or she is doing in private life to be your primary, full-time, in-home caregiver. You must consider other options.

**Many people mistakenly assume that Medicare will pay for the bulk of their long-term-care services, but it does not.** Medicare is a health-insurance program. It is designed to help people get well, heal, and improve. The goal of long-term care is not to cure an illness or condition, but rather to allow an individual the ability to attain and maintain an optimal level of day-to-day functioning.

The topic gets confusing because Medicare does cover some nursing-home costs, but there are many parameters for qualification. In the event that an individual has a condition for which he or she will need short-term care, such as rehab following surgery or care following an accident, there is a chance that he or she may qualify for some skilled-nursing benefits from Medicare.

In order to qualify to receive skilled care in a nursing facility, for instance, a patient must meet *all* of the following criteria:

- He or she must require daily skilled care that can only be provided in a skilled-nursing facility on an inpatient basis.

- He or she must be in the hospital for at least three consecutive days—not including the day of discharge—before entering a skilled-nursing facility that is certified by Medicare.

- He or she must be admitted to the skilled-nursing facility for the same condition for which he or she was treated in the hospital.

- Generally, he or she must be admitted to the skilled-nursing facility within thirty days of discharge from the hospital.

- He or she must be certified by a medical professional in the category of needing skilled nursing or skilled-rehabilitation services on a daily basis.

If an individual does meet all of the above qualifications to receive payments for a skilled-nursing home stay, his or her benefits will be paid as follows:

- Medicare pays in full all approved charges for the first twenty days.

- After day twenty, the patient will be responsible for a daily coinsurance amount of $141.50 (as of 2012).

- If the patient requires more than a hundred days of care in the skilled-nursing facility, he or she will be responsible for the entire amount due starting on day 101.

What this means is that, essentially, between days twenty-one and a hundred, even if a patient qualifies for a Medicare-approved nursing home stay, he or she is still responsible for paying a daily copayment of $141.50.

Therefore, the patient will still need to pay $11,320 ($141.50 per day over eighty days). Moreover, after day one hundred, he or she would be responsible for paying 100 percent of the charges due. It is easy to see that even with some coverage by Medicare, the cost of nursing home care can add up quickly.

Medicare will also pay some of the costs of in-home health care. If an individual needs help only with basic daily activities, Medicare will not cover these costs. However, Medicare will cover the expenses of medical care in the home, including help with daily living activities if that care falls under a doctor's orders.

In order to receive home-care coverage from Medicare, the home-care agency that is used must be Medicare approved; the patient must also meet certain qualifications of his or her Medicare, Medicare Advantage, or Medicare Supplement plan. To meet the criteria set by Medicare in order to qualify for home-care coverage, the patient must need at least one or more of the following:

- ✪ part-time nursing care
- ✪ physical therapy
- ✪ speech-language therapy
- ✪ occupational therapy

In addition, the patient must be homebound. This means that leaving the home is a major effort and the person only does it rarely, such as in order to attend church services or get medical treatment, including therapeutic or psychosocial care.

If he or she qualifies for coverage, the patient must receive home-care services from a home-health-care agency that is approved by Medicare, and/or he or she may get care in an adult-day-care program that is Medicare approved and state certified to provide adult-day-care services.

These services are typically covered by Part A or B of Medicare. Patients will pay $0 for all covered home-health visits. If the patients have a Medicare Advantage Plan or a Medicare Supplement policy, they need to contact the plan facilitator and ask about coverage, as they may need to use one of the home-care agencies that the plan lists as approved.

Seniors need to be made aware that Medicare leaves many gaps in coverage by way of coinsurance and deductibles. Even those who own

Medicare Supplement policies must understand that these policies only offer coverage that is supplemental to what Medicare covers.

So, if an individual incurs expenses that are not covered by Medicare, such as nonessential cosmetic surgery, his or her Medicare Supplement policy typically would not pay for the coinsurance or deductible. As a general rule, Medicare Supplement policies also do not cover custodial care or long-term, nursing-home, or home-health care.

**Unlike Medicare, Medicaid can pay for the bulk of nursing-home care.** However, there are stringent eligibility rules about what assets a person can have (or keep) to qualify for Medicaid benefits. In layman's terms, you have to be broke to qualify for Medicaid.

Medicaid is a needs-based welfare program. Unlike Medicare, which is run at the federal level and has a uniform benefit structure, Medicaid is administered at the state level. Even though Medicaid is a federal program, each state can interpret Medicaid qualification rules differently, a condition that can lead to conflicting and confusing decisions about people's eligibility.

In terms of qualifying for Medicaid, every state has three basic eligibility tests:

**Category test:** Applicants must be at least sixty-five years old, blind, or disabled. For most seniors needing custodial or nursing-home-care services, meeting this requirement is no problem.

**Income test:** This determines how much of the patient's income will need to be "spent down" to the nursing home. Typically, this is all income minus a personal needs allowance (in Florida, for instance, this allowance is $35 a month). Additional income rules are in place in certain states (including Florida), called "income-cap" states. In an income-cap state, if the applicant has an income greater than $2,022 a month, he or she is ineligible for Medicaid.

**Asset test:** This is how much Medicaid will allow applicants to keep. In most states, (including Florida) this is $2,000 for an individual and up to $109,000 for the well spouse.

Yep, this means there could be just $2,000 between you and the grave. This means that most middle- and upper-middle-class families face major challenges spending down, or divesting, most of the assets they have worked a lifetime to build in order to get a family member to qualify for Medicaid. It can be a heart-wrenching process.

## CAN YOU GIVE YOUR ASSETS AWAY?

In a word, no. Medicaid reviews all your financial transactions for the previous five years, known as the five-year look-back period. If Medicaid representatives find that you have given away money, property, or anything of value during that time, you will be disqualified from receiving benefits for the length of time it takes to equal the value of the gift.

For example, suppose you gave away $100,000 and then applied for Medicaid benefits. If the nursing home you were going to move into cost $5,000 a month, your disqualification period would be twenty months, or the length of time it takes to equal the $100,000 gift.

Medicaid rules and requirements go on and on—I could fill a book just about that topic. This book, however, is meant to help you plan for long-term care in such a way that you will not have to rely on Medicaid, except as a last resort.

## WHAT EXACTLY IS LONG-TERM CARE?

The term *long-term care* can mean many things, but the term can generally be defined as "the variety of services necessary for someone who requires some form of daily, ongoing assistance." The needs of an individual can range from requiring around-the-clock care to requiring some help performing a daily routine.

Often, when a medical professional is qualifying an individual for a long-term-care need, he or she will make a determination based on the patient's ability—or inability—to perform various *activities of daily living*, or ADLs. The list of ADLs includes dressing, bathing, toileting, continence, transferring (that is, walking), and eating (that is, the ability to prepare food and feed oneself).

Long-term care can be divided into various levels. These include:

- ✪ **Skilled care:** This type of care is considered to be medically necessary due to a patient's physical or mental impairment. It constitutes around-the-clock care that is provided by licensed medical professionals under the direct supervision of a physician. Although many people tend to think of this type of care as the primary type of long-term care, it really only accounts for less than 1 percent of all long-term care that is received.

- ✪ **Intermediate care:** A registered nurse (RN), licensed practical nurse (LPN), or a nurse's aide provides such care under the supervision of a physician. This care type is also considered to be medically necessary. It accounts for approximately 5 percent of all long-term care that is received.

- ✪ **Custodial care:** *Custodial care* is defined as receiving assistance with meeting daily living requirements. This refers to the receipt of supervisory or hands-on services provided to persons who suffer from a chronic illness that has been caused by a physical or cognitive impairment. This type of care is provided by a number of both professional (formal) and nonprofessional (informal) caregivers. It is not considered to be medically necessary, although the patient is not expected to recuperate from the physical or mental ailment that has caused him or her to need care. This type of care consists primarily of homemaker services, such as cleaning the house, cooking, and other types of personal-care assistance that help the individual get through his or her daily routine. Custodial care accounts for nearly 95 percent of all long-term care that is received.

An individual may need long-term care for many different reasons. He or she could have a specific illness or injury requiring him or her to receive treatment and/or rehabilitation. He or she could have a cognitive or mental impairment, such as Alzheimer's disease or other difficulties due to a stroke. Alternatively, he or she could simply require assistance with basic activities of daily living.

Impairments that require the need for long-term care can be broken down into three types, as described below.

○ **Acute impairments**: An *acute impairment* is a medical condition, such as an accident-related injury, pneumonia, or heart attack that strikes suddenly, from which the individual may fully recover with the proper medical attention. Acute impairments do not in and of themselves cause a need for long-term care. For example, a stroke is considered to be an acute impairment that, if not caught in time, could cause death. If, however, the individual survives a stroke, he or she may do so only to incur a chronic condition that actually creates the need for long-term-care services.

✪ **Physical impairment**: A *physical impairment* is a treatable, but not typically curable, chronic condition. Common examples include emphysema, arthritis, diabetes, heart disease, and hypertension. Physical impairments that require long-term care are typically expressed in terms of difficulty in performing activities of daily living.

✪ **Cognitive impairment**: A *cognitive impairment* is generally defined as a deterioration or loss of intellectual capacity as certified by a licensed health-care practitioner and measured by clinical evidence and standardized tests, which can evaluate the individual's impairment in the areas of short- or long-term memory; orientation as to person, place, or time; deductive or abstract reasoning; and judgment as it relates to awareness of safety.

✪ The individual who suffers from a cognitive impairment may be able to physically perform basic activities of daily living. However, he or she will likely need some type of supervision in doing so. Common causes of cognitive impairments include Alzheimer's disease, Parkinson's disease, and various other types of dementia. Usually, a cognitive impairment will lead to a permanent need for long-term care.

Although many people think only of skilled care when they hear the term long-term care, it is important to remember that in reality, long-term care encompasses a wide array of medical, social, personal, supportive, and specialized housing services needed by individuals who have lost some capacity for self-care due to a chronic illness or a disabling condition.

## PLANNING FOR LONG-TERM CARE

There are many different ways to plan for long-term care in your retirement income strategy. In this section, we will talk about several of them.

**Long-term-care insurance (LTCi)** is best purchased well before retirement, no later than age fifty, when it is relatively inexpensive and its qualification standards are fairly easy to meet. That way, you can figure it into your budget and plan for it throughout retirement. It will help you maintain your lifestyle, maintain your spouse's lifestyle when you pass away, and give you the peace of mind of knowing that a severe problem in life has been handled.

That said, many people simply refuse to spend money on something they may never need. They think of the premiums they will have to pay as "lost money." That kind of thinking is like saying, "Dang! I paid for automobile insurance all these years and never had a really bad wreck, so I never got my money's worth!"

What many people do not realize is that some long-term-care policies return all premiums

Benefits paid by the ten leading long-term-care insurance providers in the U.S.A. totaled nearly $4 billion in 2010, an amount that will keep growing as more aging policyholders qualify for benefits from their coverage.

paid in to a named beneficiary after the policyholder's death. That is certainly not a waste of money!

**Long-term-care planning with life insurance** is a good option for people who have accumulated some wealth. Suppose you put $100,000 in this type of policy. It will pay $5 in long-term-care benefits for every $1 you put in. It also provides $2 in death benefits for every $1 you put in. Finally, if you ever need your money back, all you need to do is ask for it. You will get 100 percent of your investment back with no penalties.

**A good universal life-insurance** policy is another no-lose way of planning for long-term care. Modern-day life-insurance policies make it possible to use some of a death benefit fund to pay for long-term care. Not only does this type of insurance protect your family with income during your working years in the event of a disability or chronic illness, but it will also provide income if you need long-term care.

Remember that even with long-term insurance, or protection through life insurance, you may still have out-of-pocket costs. As discussed in Chapter 2, these costs should be carefully factored in when estimating your retirement expenses.

Whichever way you choose to plan for long-term care, you will thank yourself in the long run. In addition to providing money for the care you may need, planning for long-term care will help you protect your assets, avoid dependency on others, and retain your dignity and freedom of choice.

## LOW INTEREST RATES MEAN LESS MONEY TO PAY OUT

The way insurance works is by investing policy-owner premiums for a conservative return. In turn, those gains are used to pay future benefits. However, due to today's prolonged low-interest-rate environment, insurance companies do not have as much money to pay out current benefits as they expected.

## RESPONSIBLE POLICY OWNERS TO BLAME

Another way insurance companies acquire money to pay out benefits is through the lapse of current policies. In the life-insurance business, about 2 percent to 4 percent of all policies are expected to lapse due to unpaid premiums. This ratio is incorporated as part of the policy-pricing formula. In recent years, however, the lapse rate has been much lower, once again leaving companies with less cash to use in paying benefits.

Given the continued lengthening of life-expectancy rates as people grow older, it is reasonable to expect a con

## LONG-TERM-CARE INSURANCE TRENDS

If you have been considering whether to buy long-term-care insurance (LTCi) or wait a while longer, you might miss out on the opportunity to buy a more benefit-rich policy. That is because many LTCi insurers are either cutting benefits in new policies sold or getting out of the business altogether.

Between 2010 and 2012, long-term-care insurance carriers Prudential, Unum, and MetLife (one of the primary underwriters of the federal government's long-term-care benefit plan) stopped selling this insurance; John Hancock and Mass Mutual ceased offering unlimited benefit periods; and Transamerica announced it was suspending limited pay options and eliminating the unlimited benefit period.

In turn, industry leader Genworth, which under-writes 40 percent of all LTCi policies sold, announced a profusion of cutbacks on previously benefit-rich policies. The Genworth changes include:

- elimination of unlimited (lifetime) benefits
- suspension of the 10-pay and pay-to-65 limited payment options
- elimination of the 10 percent preferred-health discount
- reduction of the spousal discount from 40 percent to 20 percent

Genworth will also be implementing more restrictive underwriting requirements for certain health conditions.

siderable increase in payouts in upcoming years—hence the reason many companies are exiting the business.

## PREMIUMS ON THE RISE

Insurance companies still willing to write new LTCi policies are beginning to raise premiums substantially to meet their obligations. In fact, some policies are priced at 50 percent or more than an equivalent policy would have cost ten years ago for someone of the same age. If you wait another ten years to purchase your policy, premiums may climb even higher.

Bear in mind, however, that most LTCi carriers offer other forms of insurance as well. Depending on the product portfolio, the overall company may still be in a strong financial position. Much like diversifying one's assets, a company's products that are earning higher profits help offset company losses from other products. This is why experts consistently recommend you shop around for a long-term-care insurance policy. The reality is that some carriers can still offer premiums at competitive rates and richer benefits because they are more profitable in other areas and can bear the "risk" of LTCi.

## TAX-DEDUCTIBLE PLANS

The Health Insurance Portability and Accountability Act, which passed in 1997, made some or all of the premiums of federally qualified policies deductible as a medical expense on federal income-tax returns (subject to the filer's age and the amount of the annual premium). You should speak with an experienced tax advisor regarding the tax deductibility of LTCi premiums in reference to your situation.

The following are questions you should address when considering whether to purchase an LTCi policy:

- ✪ What services and types of care does the policy cover?

- ✪ Who can provide the care? Where? (Is the care at home or in a facility? What type of facility?)

- ✪ What conditions need to be met before the issuer will pay and/or reimburse the cost of benefits?

- ✪ What are the coverage maximums and/or limits?

- ✪ Does the plan have an elimination period (also referred to as a *waiting period* or *deductible period*)?

- ✪ Does the policy offer inflation-protected benefits?

- ✪ What are the financial-strength and stability ratings of the policy issuer?

Note that federally qualified LTCi policies offer certain protections; for example, the insurer may not cancel coverage unless you fail to pay premiums on time (this means your coverage may not be cancelled because of your age or health status). In addition, if you can no longer afford the premium for the coverage you have bought, you have the right to reduce your benefits in return for a lower premium. Reduced benefits may include a lower daily benefit or fewer years that the company will pay benefits.

[END OF CHAPTER WRAP-UP]

# PREPARE FOR A LONG-TERM DETOUR

⊕ As people live longer, the likelihood increases that at some point they will need to have in-home care or move to an assisted-living facility or nursing home. In fact, 70 percent of Americans over sixty-five will need long-term-care services at some point. This dreaded possibility and its substantial financial consequences are risks that cannot be ignored.

⊕ Medicare is a health-insurance program, not a long-term-care insurance program. It is designed to help us get well, to heal, and to improve. The goal of long-term care is not to cure an illness or condition, but rather to allow an individual the ability to attain and maintain an optimal level of day-to-day functioning.

⊕ Medicaid can pay for the bulk of nursing home costs, but applicants have to be impoverished to qualify for it. This means that many seniors have to "spend down," or divest, the assets they have worked a lifetime to build. Only as a last resort would I recommend Medicaid as a funding source for long-term care.

⊕ There are many ways to plan for long-term care in your retirement income strategy:

- traditional long-term-care insurance

- long-term-care planning with life insurance

- universal life insurance in which some of the death benefit may be used to pay for long-term care

⊕ Even if you have long-term care coverage, you may still incur significant out-of-pocket long-term-care costs. This eventuality must be factored carefully into your retirement income plan.

*Chapter 7:*

# PLANNING
# FOR THE END
# OF THE ROAD

DO YOURSELF AND YOUR LOVED ONES A FAVOR BY MAKING
YOUR ESTATE DECISIONS SOONER RATHER THAN LATER.

E ven when individuals work hard their entire lives to accumulate wealth and provide for their families, all of their hard work can come to an end in an instant if they fail to plan properly.

Estate planning can really be considered lifetime planning. It should focus on planning for life, as well as for death. This includes not only the life of the individual, but also the lives of family members, loved ones, and heirs. This type of planning involves setting out financial and tax matters, while also making sure that loved ones will be secure. Like any other aspect of retirement planning, when undergoing estate planning you need to know the facts, understand your options, and work with a trained professional to help translate your individual needs and priorities into a workable strategy.

Many people think that drafting a simple will is all they need to do in the area of estate planning. Actually, estate planning is much more complex than that. Throughout this chapter, I will explain some of the basics of estate planning; I will start with the foundation documents and move on from there.

## DURABLE POWER OF ATTORNEY (POA)

A *durable power of attorney* can help protect your property in the event you become physically unable or mentally incompetent to handle financial matters. If no one is ready to look after your financial affairs when you cannot do so, your property may be wasted, abused, or lost. A durable power of attorney allows you to authorize someone else to act on your behalf, so he or she can do things such as pay bills, collect benefits, watch over your investments, and file taxes.

Without a power of attorney, the interested party must begin legal proceedings to become legal guardian.

## ADVANCE MEDICAL DIRECTIVES

*Advance medical directives* let others know what medical treatment you would want, or allow someone to make medical decisions for you, in the event you cannot express your wishes yourself. If you do not have an advance medical directive, medical-care providers must prolong your life using artificial means, if necessary.

There are three types of advance medical directives:

- ✪ A **living will** allows you to approve or decline certain types of medical care, even if you will die as a result of that choice. In most states, living wills take effect only under certain circumstances, such as terminal injury or illness. Generally, a living will can be used only to decline medical treatment that "serves only to postpone the moment of death." In those states that do not allow living wills, you may still want to have one to serve as evidence of your wishes.

- ✪ A **durable power of attorney for health care** (known as a health-care proxy in some states) allows you to appoint a representative to make medical decisions for you. You decide how much power your representative will or will not have.

- ✪ A **do-not-resuscitate order** (DNR) is a doctor's order instructing medical personnel not to perform CPR if you go into cardiac arrest. There are two types of DNRs: one is effective only while you are hospitalized, and the other is used if you are not in a hospital.

## LAST WILL AND TESTAMENT

A will is often said to be the cornerstone of any estate plan. The main purpose of a will is to disburse property to your heirs after you die. If you do not leave a will, disbursements will be made according to state law, which may or may not align with your wishes. There are two other equally important aspects of a will:

✪ You can name the person (executor) who will manage and settle your estate. If you do not name someone, the court will appoint an administrator.

✪ You can nominate a legal guardian for minor children or dependents with special needs. If you do not appoint a guardian, the state will appoint one for you.

Keep in mind that a will is a legal document, and the courts are very reluctant to overturn any provisions within it. Therefore, it is crucial that your will be clearly written and articulated, and properly executed under your state's laws. It is also important to keep your will up-to-date.

As of 2007, 55 percent of all adult Americans did not have a will.

Dying without a will, or dying *intestate*, means that you have no say over who receives your assets and your estate must go through probate. This leaves your heirs and the court system the complex and costly job of wrangling over which individual(s) should get what.

## HOW DOES PROBATE WORK?

Quite simply, probate is a mess. When you die, your heirs must go to probate court and petition the court to "be allowed" to use your assets. The heirs must report to the court the assets that have come in, the assets that have gone out, and to whom the assets are distributed. All of the information about your estate is made publicly available.

Probate court can become quite expensive due to the length and detail of the process. Your heirs or beneficiaries will incur the court costs involved with going through probate court, and, in most cases, they will also require the assistance of a lawyer, which means additional attorney costs.

One of the primary reasons people leave money to their loved ones is to help pay the bills that funerals and burials will incur. If your heirs are faced with probate court, they will not have immediate access to the funds or assets that you leave behind. As a result, the onus is then put on your loved ones to pay for your funeral expenses before they have access to your funds. Until petition is made in probate court, they will also be responsible for paying your debts to creditors after you have passed on.

Even after petition is made in probate court, the process tends to drag out longer than anyone expects. In fact, the average time in probate court is well over a year. Can you imagine looking down on your loved ones as they are forced to deal with your funeral expenses and your debts, all while going through a year or more of probate court? The best way to deal with probate is to avoid it altogether.

In 1989, the American Association of Retired Persons (AARP) decided to look carefully at probate and its impact on Seniors. As the organization reported in its study *Probate: Consumer Prospectives and Concerns,* probate is a special concern for older Americans.

The study found that 90 percent of all probate cases involved the disposition of property owned by people 60 years of age or older. Because the chances of becoming incapacitated increase dramatically as we age, living probate is also much more likely to involve seniors.

AARP went on to reveal that consumers nationally spend as much as $2 billion or more each year on probate-related expenses, with attorneys' fees alone representing more than $1.5 billion of that amount. The study noted that attorney's and executor's fees could consume as much as 20 percent of small estates, and as much as 10 percent of even uncomplicated estates. And that's only the beginning. Add to these fees such expenses as court costs and appraisers' fees, and your heirs could end up with a legacy that's considerably less than you intended.

Unreasonable expenses aren't probate's only drawbacks. There's also the time involved. AARP's study found that probate frequently lasts longer than a year. Having a will seemed to make no difference in the time required. In fact, it could drag the process out even longer.

Now, add to the expenses and delays of probate these problems: a loss of control over one's affairs and the publicity it requires. You can see why AARP declared that: "Probate as it is generally practiced in the United States is an anachronism…and, to the extent that the probate system is unreasonable, attorneys' fees in connection with probate work are unreasonable."

AARP's edict sums up the reason for so much rancor between pro-probate and pro-trust attorneys. It's a matter of money, and loss of it. The AARP study noted that attorneys often build lucrative practices focused solely on probate. Many use cheap wills as a "loss leader."

According to AARP: "This marketing practice may set a costly trap for consumers. Attorneys lay the groundwork for their probate practice by writing wills. Some write wills cheaply as a way to generate other business, prompting the comparison to loss leader discounts in the retail trade. When the client later dies, the same attorney, or another member of the firm, probates the will at a fee high enough to recover any money lost on the earlier discount."

"Death Probate" has these primary functions:

- ✪ It verifies the validity of your will.

- ✪ It inventories and establishes the value of your significant assets.

- ✪ It gives disgruntled family members a forum for challenging your will.

- ✪ Lastly, when all these steps have been completed, it transfers the title of your property to your heirs, as you've instructed in your will.

Do you really need probate to accomplish these tasks? AARP says no. Instead, it recommends alternatives such as the Revocable Living Trust.

## TRUST BASICS

A trust does not pass away; a trust does not die. A trust is a living document; it is a legal entity that lets you put conditions on how certain assets are distributed upon your death. In addition, trusts can help minimize gift and estate taxes. Another benefit is that trusts are not public documents.

A properly written and funded trust can save time, money, and headaches for your loved ones as they deal with your death. Your trustee can access funds to pay for funeral expenses and/or debts that you leave, and then he or she can distribute the assets in accordance with your last will and testament.

There are many different kinds of trusts, each applying to specific situations. An experienced retirement income planner and estate attorney can help you establish one (or more) that fit(s) your needs.

## REVOCABLE LIVING TRUSTS

A *revocable living trust*, also referred to as a *revocable trust* or *living trust*, is a type of trust that can be changed at any time. In other words, if you have second thoughts about a provision in the trust or change your mind about a trust beneficiary or fiduciary, you can modify the terms of the trust through what is termed a *trust amendment*. Alternatively, if you decide that you do not like anything about the trust at all, you can either revoke the entire agreement or change the contents through an amendment and restatement.

Since revocable living trusts are so flexible, why aren't all trusts revocable? The downside to a revocable trust is that assets funded into the trust are still considered your own personal assets for creditor and estate-tax purposes. This means that a revocable trust offers no creditor protection if you are sued, and all assets held in the name of the trust at the time of your death will be subject to both state and federal estate taxes.

You should use a revocable living trust as part of your estate plan for three reasons, as discussed below:

**To plan for mental disability:** Assets held in the name of a revocable living trust at the time a person becomes mentally incapacitated can be managed by that person's disability trustee rather than a court-supervised guardian or conservator.

**To avoid probate:** Assets held in the name of a revocable living trust at the time of a person's death will pass directly to the beneficiaries named in the trust agreement without going through probate.

**To keep information about your property and beneficiaries private:** By avoiding probate with a revocable living trust, your trust agreement will not become a public record for all the world to see, which means the details about your assets and beneficiaries will be kept private. Contrast this with a last will and testament that has been admitted to probate. Such a will becomes a public court record that anyone can read.

## IRREVOCABLE TRUSTS

An *irrevocable trust* is simply a type of trust that cannot be changed after the agreement has been signed. A typical revocable living trust becomes irrevocable when the trust maker dies, and it can be designed to break into separate irrevocable trusts for the benefit of a surviving spouse or into multiple irrevocable lifetime trusts for the benefit of children or other beneficiaries.

Irrevocable trusts can take on many forms and be used to accomplish a variety of estate-planning goals:

**Estate tax reduction:** Irrevocable trusts, such as *irrevocable life-insurance trusts*, are commonly used to remove the value of property from a person's estate so the property cannot be taxed when the trust maker dies. In other words, the person who transfers assets into an irrevocable trust is giving over those assets to the trustee and beneficiaries of the trust so that person no longer owns the assets. Thus, if that person no longer owns the assets, the estate cannot be taxed when he or she later dies.

*AB trusts* created for the benefit of a surviving spouse are irrevocable and thereby can make full use of the deceased spouse's exemption from estate taxes through the funding of the B trust with property valued at or below the estate tax exemption. If the value of the deceased spouse's estate exceeds the estate-tax exemption, the A trust will be funded for the benefit of the surviving spouse, and payment of estate taxes will be deferred until after the surviving spouse dies.

*ABC trusts* can be used by married couples living in some of the states that collect a state estate tax, when the state estate-tax exemption is less than the federal estate-tax exemption. For example, in Massachusetts the state estate-tax exemption is only $1 million, as compared with the current federal exemption of $5 million. So, in Massachusetts, a couple's first $1 million goes into the B trust, the next $4 million goes into the C trust, and anything over $5 million goes into the A trust.

**Asset protection:** Another common use for an irrevocable trust is to provide asset protection for the trust maker and the trust maker's family. This works in the same way that an irrevocable trust can work to reduce estate taxes. By placing assets into an irrevocable trust, the trust maker gives up complete control over, and access to, the trust assets; therefore, creditors cannot reach the trust assets. However, the trust maker's family can be the beneficiaries of the irrevocable trust, thereby still providing the family with financial support that is outside the creditors' reach.

In some states, including Alaska, Delaware, Nevada, and Tennessee, there are also irrevocable trusts known as *self-settled trusts*, or *domestic-asset-protection trusts*, that offer creditor protection and allow the trust maker to be a trust beneficiary.

**Charitable estate planning:** Another common use of an irrevocable trust is to accomplish charitable estate planning, usually through a *charitable remainder* trust or a *charitable lead trust*. If the trust maker makes the initial transfer of assets into a charitable trust while still alive, he or she will receive a charitable income-tax deduction in the year the transfer is made. Alternatively, if the initial transfer of assets into a charitable trust does not occur until after the trust maker's death, the trust maker's estate will receive a charitable estate-tax deduction.

The following are a few more examples of irrevocable living trusts:

**Dynasty trusts:** Long-term *dynasty trusts* are created to pass wealth from generation to generation without incurring transfer taxes such as estate and gift taxes. The dynasty trust's defining characteristic is its term. The trust can survive for twenty-one years after the death of the last beneficiary who was alive when the trust was set up, so it can easily last for more than one hundred years. The beneficiaries of a dynasty trust are usually the trust maker's children. After the death of the last child, the trust maker's grandchildren or great-grandchildren generally become the beneficiaries. The trustee who is appointed by the trust maker controls the trust's operation. The dynasty trust is irrevocable, which means that once it is funded, the trust maker will not have any control over the assets or be permitted to amend the trust terms.

**Spendthrift trusts:** If you are worried about your beneficiaries spending all your assets in one place, you might want to consider this type of trust. The *spendthrift trust* is designed to deliver benefits to beneficiaries on an as-needed basis. Rather than providing instant access to all of the funds, you can prolong the benefits you leave while protecting the money from creditors.

**QTIP trusts:** A *qualified terminable interest property trust*, or QTIP, is an effective tool for blended families that result from more than one marriage. For example, a QTIP trust can provide income for a spouse from a second marriage and then pass on remaining proceeds to the children from the first marriage after the second spouse dies. Otherwise, the surviving spouse may have all remaining assets pass on to his or her own children (from a previous marriage) upon death, rather than to the original decedent's children.

In a marital trust, a portion of the trust is fully accessible by the surviving spouse. However, a QTIP trust provides a surviving spouse only limited access. He or she may receive income from the trust but may not withdraw principal or decide how the assets are delineated at death, when the trust is distributed according to the original decedent's wishes.

## CHOOSING AN EXECUTOR AND/OR A TRUSTEE

Who should be the executor, or the trustee, of your estate? It should be someone you trust completely (no pun intended). Beyond that, here are some other elements you should consider:

- Does the person want the job? Discuss it with him or her to make sure he or she is willing to take on this responsibility.

- Does the person live near where the estate will be settled? A long-distance commute is not a deal breaker, but having the executor live locally can make things much more convenient for the parties involved.

- Sometimes there is not a family member who is available or appropriate for the task. In such cases, you might want to consider naming a professional trustee, such as your retirement planner.

## FILL-IN-THE-BLANK ESTATE PLANS

Much estate planning has been reduced to a commodity service because many people think of estate planning as just buying and filling in some cheap, fill-in-the-blank documents. This mindset can also lead to hiring a cheap, fill-in-the-blank lawyer, which almost always results in the validation of the timeworn saying, "You get what you pay for."

If you purchase fill-in-the-blank estate documents and complete them yourself, then you are the lawyer. If you choose a cheap, fill-in-the-blank lawyer, you can expect him or her to devote as little time and talent as possible in order to deliver a cookie-cutter estate plan.

One of the most important steps in estate planning is funding clients' trusts. *Trust funding* means changing the title ownership of real estate, the beneficiary designation of policies and annuities, the names on brokerage accounts, and the ownership of all other assets to fit the estate plan. Hours of labor must be invested to ensure that the plan will fulfill the trust maker's goals after death. A fill-in-the-blank estate plan simply does not provide the level of detail necessary to fund a trust properly; often, it results in chaos and an enormous legal fee to do the cleanup work.

### WILLS, TRUSTS, OR BENEFICIARY FORMS: WHICH RULES?

Here is an interesting story for you. A guy (we will call him "Sam") was married to a gal (we will call her "Sue") for many years. Then they got divorced. In the divorce agreement, Sue gave up all rights to Sam's 401(k) plan and life insurance. Sam changed his will and trust to name his children as beneficiaries of all of his assets, but he never changed the beneficiary of either his 401(k) or his life insurance. Sue remained listed on those documents.

Then Sam died. After his death, a problem emerges: Who should get the money from his 401(k) and his life insurance? Do his children get the money because they are named as his beneficiaries in his will and trust? Or should Sue get the money because she is named as beneficiary of his life insurance and his 401(k)? (Remember, she signed off all rights to this money in the divorce agreement.)

Answer: Sue would get the money.

Why would Sue receive the funds? She would get the money because beneficiary agreements trump wills and trusts. The Supreme Court has ruled in multiple cases, usually 9–0, that beneficiary forms override all others, with some exceptions (which I will explain later on in this chapter).

Now, let's change the facts a bit. Assume that Sam also changed the beneficiary forms on his life insurance and 401(k), and named his children as beneficiaries. Who would get the money then?

In this case, the children would get the money as expected.

One more change to the facts. Imagine Sam got remarried to Sally. His children were still listed as the beneficiaries on both his life insurance and his 401(k). He was married to Sally for six months, and then died. Who would get the money then?

Answer: The children would get the life insurance and Sally would likely get his 401(k), even though the children are listed as beneficiaries.

How can this be?

This is because 401(k) plans are *ERISA* plans, which require the spouse to be the beneficiary, unless the spouse has signed a waiver giving up the rights to the money. Odds are very high that Sam would never have had his wife sign that form. Since Sally was Sam's wife at the time of his death, ERISA regulations say she would get the money, and not the children.

Had Sam moved his money into an IRA, which is a non-ERISA plan, it would have gone to the children, as he had wished.

..........................................................................................

# PLANNING FOR THE END OF THE ROAD

✪ The most important estate-planning documents are:

- durable power of attorney

- advance medical directive(s)

- last will and testament

- irrevocable living trust and/or revocable trust(s)

Get your estate documents in order; then, relax and enjoy life!

✪ It is important to let your wishes be known in these documents, so they can speak for you when you no longer can.

✪ You want to avoid having your estate go through probate, which can be a tedious, time-consuming, and expensive process for your family.

✪ There are many types of trusts that can be used to minimize tax consequences to your heirs and to achieve a number of other estate-planning goals. Your retirement planner and estate lawyer can help you set up the right trust(s) for your particular situation.

✪ Keep your account beneficiary forms and estate documents up to date, reflecting family changes or a change in your selected executor(s) or trustee(s).

# Chapter 8:

# ROADSIDE ASSISTANCE

EVEN THE BEST PLANS NEED ADJUSTING FROM TIME TO TIME. A TRUSTED RETIREMENT PLANNER WILL MONITOR YOUR PROGRESS AND MAKE ANY NECESSARY MIDCOURSE ALTERATIONS TO KEEP YOUR RETIREMENT ON TRACK.

I once heard a man ask a minister what kind of oil would be best to put on the leather cover of his Bible. The minister looked at him and said, "Palm oil." The minister did not mean the oil from palm trees; instead, he meant the oil from hands regularly opening and holding the book. In other words, he meant the man should visit the Bible frequently; go to it on a regular basis.

Your retirement plan probably does not have a leather cover on it, but I recommend you season it with plenty of palm oil, nonetheless. Even the best plan in the world needs monitoring and tweaking from time to time, and a good retirement-income planner will sit down with you regularly—at least once a year—to make sure your plan is still on course.

You may need revisions to wills and trusts, for example, or there may be steps you can take to reduce taxes. Perhaps you could be using debt more wisely or allocating your assets among investment classes to achieve greater returns while reducing risk. Maybe your family or work situation has changed, or someone in your immediate family is having some health problems. You could be thinking about moving or selling an income property.

Of course, you do not need your advisor's permission to attend to these things. However, having a quick chat with him or her before making any moves that have significant financial implications is certainly worthwhile. After all, you want your retirement roadmap to be as accurate and up-to-date as possible.

If you have not yet found a retirement-income planner to help you chart out your retirement roadmap, here are a few pointers.

## FINDING THE RIGHT ADVISOR

This is where the rubber meets the road. Getting the right advice will make all the difference in your retirement income plan. Will you choose to protect your retirement and your income, or will you roll the dice?

I cannot stress enough the importance of the topics I have raised throughout this book. I hope that you take the knowledge you have garnered and put it to good use in making smarter decisions with your hard-earned money.

Do you believe that knowledge is power? You do, right? Well, that is only partially true. The *application* of knowledge is what is powerful.

The first step on this journey is up to you. You need to find a financial professional who will help guide you through the daunting and uncertain terrain of retirement income planning. The following are seven steps you can take to find a retirement income planner who will assist you in developing a plan that works for you. By following these steps, you will find someone who fits your needs. Read through them. They could save your financial life.

## DO NOT DO IT ALONE

You need to find someone who specializes in retirement income planning and, if possible, tax planning. This person should work closely with a qualified estate attorney, registered investment advisor, licensed insurance producer, and an accountant. These professionals should share a like mindset with each other and with you.

You might be thinking, "Why can't I do all the things you talked about in this book myself?"

While some people do succeed in planning their retirement on their own, several things tend to get in the way, such as emotional attachment to their own money or not having the proper licenses to access certain products or investments.

The ones who find the best retirement routes are the folks who seek out assistance from a team of like-minded professionals who specialize in asset preservation and distribution planning. Together, you and your team can develop a winning strategy that encompasses all of your retirement goals and objectives.

## IF IT SOUNDS TOO GOOD TO BE TRUE, IT PROBABLY IS

Watch out for financial "salespeople." Many of them—including brokers and bankers—like to pose as "financial advisors." Unfortunately, rather than advising you on what you should be doing with your money to meet your goals, they are simply selling you a product. There is a fine line you can draw that will help you determine if you could be falling victim to this. Use these questions to figure it out:

- ✪ Is the advisor a fiduciary? As we discussed in Chapter 5, some advisors are merely held to a *suitability* standard, which means they need only find you a product that is suitable for your situation. Being a fiduciary means that, by law, the advisor must find the best product available for your needs, and your needs must come before his or her own.

- ✪ **Did the advisor ask the right questions?** Did the advisor spend time with you, asking important questions about what you want your money to do for you? Questions are important. Simply reading the answers to a risk questionnaire is not a reliable way to recommend an investment product. Your advisor should know exactly what your goals and objectives are for every investment piece of your retirement portfolio puzzle. Most importantly, your expectations of the investment should be in line with the advice.

- ✪ **Does the advisor team up with the right specialists?** One quick way to determine if you are dealing with a financial salesperson is to take a hard look at his or her team. With whom does he or she work? Does he or she work alone? Does he or she have employees? Does he or she only work with securities? Does he or she only work with insurance products? Does he or she work with qualified estate attorneys and/or tax planners?

✪ **Is he or she pushing for too-rapid decisions?** The telltale sign that a financial advisor is nothing but a salesperson is if he or she tries to sell you a product versus a plan. An advisor should take the time that is necessary to get to know you, ask you the proper questions, go over all of your problems and concerns, and then draft a plan of attack to address your goals and objectives.

The last part is how to fund this plan of attack. Funding your plan is merely a process of reallocating your money to new investments that better suit your situation. There are a lot of great financial products available to you that you might not already know about, but remember that most great products come with strings attached. Make sure you understand fully what you are being offered and the strings attached to each option.

✪ **Does the advisor follow a professional code of ethics?** Anyone who is handling your personal finances should be accountable to a professional code of ethics. Of course, no code of ethics can guarantee you will get good service or great investment results. Following such a code does indicate, however, that the person managing your assets most likely has your best interests at heart. The following is the code of ethics for the International Association of Registered Financial Consultants, which we observe in my office:

  ▫ I will at all times put my clients' interests above my own.

- I will maintain proficiency in my work through continuing education.

- I will abide by both the spirit and the letter of the laws and regulations applicable to financial-planning services.

- When fee-based services are involved, I will charge a fair and reasonable fee based on the amount of time and skill required.

- I will give my clients the same service I would give myself in the same circumstances.

## WATCH OUT FOR COMMISSION BROKERS

How is your advisor getting paid? Do you think you have received enough value for the amount that you are paying? In other words, is the fee you are paying worth the advice you are getting?

## BEWARE OF ONLINE "RESOURCES"

Be careful about doing research online. It has become increasingly common to find the answers for anything these days by typing your question into Google. That does not mean, however, that the answer you find is the right one. For example, I recently typed the phrase "retirement-income planning" into Google, and 24.3 million results came up. That is information overload, and it can be a huge problem.

If you are going to do research online, you should be spending time researching a team of professionals who can help you. Focus your efforts on finding a retirement-income planner who can meet your needs: someone who specializes in retirement income, preservation of assets, and estate planning.

## DEMAND PROOF

Financial salespeople can be very swift talkers. They may sound like the real deal, but are they? You need to demand proof. Ask them the following questions. Their answers should give you some insight as to whether or not you are working with a true expert.

- ✪ **Have you ever been published in an industry periodical or featured in the financial media?** The top financial media outlets want their viewers and readers to get credible and accurate information. Both you and the financial media need someone who does not just talk a good game, but also really knows his or her stuff.

- ✪ **Have you written a book on your subject?** Even though there are financial professionals who are not authors but are still credible sources, professionals who take time to write about their trade are clearly passionate about what they do. It is not easy to write a book, trust me. However, professionals who are proud of the service they provide often have a published book to back it up.

- ✪ **Do you invest in your professional knowledge?** This is a good gauge of how current your advisor is with reference to the economy, tax code changes, new laws, and cutting-edge ideas and planning strategies.

  Our world is constantly changing. If advisors are not investing in their own education, odds are that they are bringing old ideas and strategies to the table.

- ✪ **Do other professionals trust you to help their clients?** I am not talking about simple references here. When other professionals (estate attorneys, accountants, insurance specialists, and so on) refer their clients to this advisor, it means they trust the advisor to do the right thing for their clients. That is a big endorsement.

## AVOID COOKIE-CUTTER FINANCIAL PLANS

Cookie cutters are for making cookies, not retirement plans. I think one of the largest problems and hidden truths about financial advisors is that many do not create plans customized to clients' unique goals and concerns. These financial salespeople use cookie-cutter plans hidden carefully within clever sales and marketing pitches with the intent of making you believe such a plan was made just for you.

The financial plans from some of the biggest, best-advertised brokerage and mutual-fund houses are often just the same plans peddled over and over without regard to the individual's goals, concerns, and problems. There is a real difference between investing and planning, and what you need at this stage of life is a plan as unique as your fingerprints.

To help make sure you do not end up with a cookie-cutter plan, be sure to ask some tough questions. Here is a short list to help you get started:

- ✪ How does my plan differ from your other clients' plans?
- ✪ Do you rely on others to make buy and/or sell decisions on my investments?
- ✪ Has your parent company ever been sued for selling cookie-cutter plans?

✪ Do you have special selling agreements with outside investment companies that offer you bigger payouts for using their products?

## TRUST YOUR FEELINGS

Much is revealed when you meet face-to-face with a potential advisor. See how you feel. When you walk through the door, you need to be treated as if you are a member of that practice's family. If you feel more comfortable and secure about your future after talking to a particular advisor, then you might be in the right place.

At the beginning of this book, I congratulated you for starting to take action toward planning financially for your retirement. Now that you have read the book, do you feel better prepared to embark on that journey? I certainly hope so.

As we have discussed, we live in a fast-moving world abuzz with constant change. For regular updates about retirement planning, I invite you to listen to my radio show, *The Financial Safari,* which is broadcast on Saturday mornings at 11 a.m. CST on WCOA AM 1370 and WEBY AM 1330. I also publish a weekly newsletter that you can sign up for at my website: www.safeharbortaxadvisory.com. Better yet, come see me when you are in the Pensacola area.

Keep up the momentum you have gotten going through reading this book to take control of your financial future and start putting a failsafe plan in place that will provide you with guaranteed lifetime retirement income. Nothing beats being able to stop worrying about your retirement and start enjoying it.

I wish you all the best in finding the right guide and enjoying the wonderful adventure you have been working toward all these years.

Don Moore,
*Registered Financial Consultant®,*
*Certified Estate and Trust Specialist™*
*Investment Advisor Representative and Fiduciary*
*850-435-4844*
*Safe Harbor Tax Advisory, LLC*
*25 West Cedar Street, Suite 110*
*Pensacola, FL 32502*
*don@safeharbortaxadvisory.com*
*www.safeharbortaxadvisory.com*

...................................................................................................................

[END OF CHAPTER WRAP-UP]

# ROADSIDE ASSISTANCE

✪ On the road to retirement, and even after you arrive at your destination, it is very likely that your roadmap may need updating. A good retirement planner does the following:

- monitors the results of your investments to make sure they perform as originally projected

- adjusts insurance coverage as needed

- stays abreast of tax codes and continually applies reduction techniques

- facilitates revisions to your wills, trusts, legal powers, and directives

- continues to help you use debt wisely and reduce it to increase security

- acts on your decisions to alter original retirement plans

✪ How do you find such a planner? Here are some pointers. Your guide should:

- be a fiduciary

- specialize in retirement-income planning

- ask the right questions

- team up with the right specialists

- invest in ongoing professional knowledge

- be recommended by other professionals

- provide proof of expertise

- feel like a good fit to you

✪ Best wishes for a wonderful retirement journey!

# ABOUT THE AUTHOR

**N**ow that you have read my book, I suppose I should tell you a little about myself and my practice, which is based in Pensacola, Fla., on the Gulf of Mexico's beautiful Emerald Coast. My marketing materials say something like, "Donald Moore, RFC®, CES™, is a veteran of the industry and one of the most successful retirement planners in the northwest Florida and southwest Alabama area." I love what I do because I have been able to help many terrific people stop worrying about their retirement and start enjoying it.

I specialize in creating innovative tax and investment solutions to help clients achieve their goals in retirement. This may include strategies to create significant tax reductions on retirement plans, thereby leaving more money available for their enjoyment. Alternatively, it could mean portfolio optimization techniques that guarantee principal while simultaneously maximizing growth opportunities. It might also include failsafe retirement-income strategies that guarantee income while keeping tax liability to a minimum.

The strategies we employ must produce the desired effect. The ultimate outcome must be to protect the client's investment while making his or her desired retirement lifestyle possible.

As described in the book, the biggest challenge I face when dealing with clients is mindset. There has to be a mindset change when a person enters retirement. When it comes to a client's financial investments, he or she must change from a growth-and-accumulation mode to a preservation mode. My expertise is in helping clients understand the need for that kind of portfolio shift.

I only work with retirees and preretirees who fit a very specific profile. At my practice, we usually have an initial meeting so the prospective client can determine if our strategies are a fit for him or her, and for us to determine if the prospective client is a fit for us. On some occasions, I have had to tell a prospective client that the relationship would not be a good fit and he or she should seek an investment advisor who lines up more closely with his or her objectives.

Why am I so strict about my postretirement strategy? I have always believed that during a person's working years he or she should be in an accumulation mindset of investing. One day, all of us would like to retire; during our working years, our main purpose in investing is to accumulate as much in assets as possible so we can retire. When we retire, however, we have made the money we are going to make during our lifetime, and our investing mindset should switch from an accumulation mode to a preservation mode.

To me, nothing is worse than the promise of retirement devastated by risky investing. I have developed my own strategies that focus on the preservation of assets and protecting investment portfolios through intelligent tax planning. Applying these strategies has proven successful for hundreds of clients over the years.

A fully integrated retirement plan must include an income plan, an investment plan, a tax plan, a health-care plan, and an estate plan. However, most people do not have a complete plan in any one of those areas, let alone all five. With pensions disappearing and portfolios wearing thin in the recession, 90 percent of my new clients' primary concern is this: "How can we take our accounts and use them to generate secure, sustainable lifetime income regardless of what the markets do?" Clients are more scared of running out of money than they are of dying.

I follow four primary principles that I believe are the foundation of my practice's success:

- First, I specialize in a market, and I pay very close attention to that target market.

- Second, I continuously work on improving what I do and how I do it.

- Third, I remain very objective and open-minded, and am always willing to use different tools. I continue to attend industry events to expand my education in this field.

- Finally, I do not try to attract people who do not fit the model I have found to be very successful. In other words, I do not try to fit a square peg in a round hole.

Along with my financial advisory firm, Safe Harbor Fiduciary Advisors, LLC, I am also the founder and principal of Safe Harbor Tax Advisory, LLC; the latter firm specializes in preparing tax returns for retired individuals and couples. As you can guess from reading the chapter on taxes in this book, at my firm we are dedicated to ensuring that our clients pay the lowest possible tax allowed by the IRS.

I am a Registered Financial Consultant®, and a Certified Estate and Trust Specialist™. I also host my own financial-planning radio program on five radio stations in northwest Florida and southwest Alabama, and I teach retirement-planning classes at the University of West Florida.

In my spare time I enjoy fishing, hunting, golfing, hiking, and just about any outdoor activity.

It is my fervent desire that this book assists you in making your retirement as wonderful as you hoped it would be. Retirement is a wonderful place to live if you can afford it...

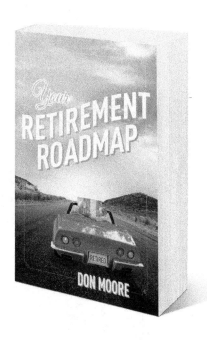

# How can you use this book?

MOTIVATE

EDUCATE

THANK

INSPIRE

PROMOTE

CONNECT

## Why have a custom version of *Your Retirement Roadmap?*

✪ Build personal bonds with customers, prospects, employees, donors, and key constituencies

✪ Develop a long-lasting reminder of your event, milestone, or celebration

✪ Provide a keepsake that inspires change in behavior and change in lives

✪ Deliver the ultimate "thank you" gift that remains on coffee tables and bookshelves

✪ Generate the "wow" factor

Books are thoughtful gifts that provide a genuine sentiment that other promotional items cannot express. They promote employee discussions and interaction, reinforce an event's meaning or location, and they make a lasting impression. Use your book to say "Thank You" and show people that you care.

*Your Retirement Roadmap* is available in bulk quantities and in customized versions at special discounts for corporate, institutional, and educational purposes. To learn more please contact our Special Sales team at:

**1.866.775.1696 • sales@advantageww.com • www.AdvantageSpecialSales.com**

9 781599 323688